What was I Thinking?

What was I Thinking?

Kent McClain

Ralph   Wendell   Kent

Learning an ocean of grace in a pond of legalism

Dedicated to my brother, Jerry, and great friend, Ralph

Copyright 2018 Destinée Media Publishing

Preface

The stories I am about to tell may make you laugh at times, for several episodes are funny, and they may cause you to wonder if I am making them up! This amusing collection of stories is based on real events and not created just to make an exciting book. What I am about to share happened between the years of 1964 and 1968 on a Christian college campus in Southern California. The college was Pasadena Nazarene College or what was frequently called Paz Naz or PC.

These were some of the greatest years to be a young person, especially in liberal Southern California. There were hardly any real pressures about which to worry. The economy was strong; gas was 25 cents a gallon; jobs were plentiful; housing was cheap; and new freedoms were open to be tested, such as the anti-establishment, or hippie movement. To just get a B.A. degree insured financial security, but then to go on and complete an M.A., which a few of us pursued, only added to one's prestige and potential.

The hippie and Jesus movements during this era were growing. These brought a real breath of fresh air to all young people, even to a PC student like me.

Generally, churches during these years were out of step with these movements because they did not fully comprehend the changes taking place with young people during this era. The

Nazarene denomination, similar to others like it, too often practiced a Christianity that emphasized what a Christian should look like on the outside and paid less attention to spiritual transformation within.

The story of PC is multifaceted because it reveals the many struggles students experienced while attending a rule-oriented Christian college in the 60s. Some students came to PC of their own choice, wanting a small Christian college education; others came to play sports, but most came because of the influence of their parents and church.

The inspiration behind writing this narrative began with a conversation I had with my daughter, wife, and several friends. Over the years, they picked up bits and pieces of the PC story, but on this one evening, they began to laugh and even wonder if I was exaggerating. My daughter, Shannon, said, "Dad, you have to write a book about this."

What you read in this PC story is fundamentally true, with some embellishments and reinterpretations. Where my memory failed me as to the exact sequence of a few events, I wrote as best I could recollect what had happened. I also changed names to protect the reputations of individuals and not negate positive changes that may have occurred over time in each life. As Sergeant Friday used to say in the TV series *Dragnet* during that era, "The names have been changed to protect the innocent."

In essence, this is a unique story filled with a lot of humor, frustration, resolve, and truth. In the end, God's grace won out and took root in my life, which is the main reason I wrote this book. I hope you enjoy it.

Finally, even though I express a measure of criticism in these stories toward some of the Nazarene doctrines, practices, and leaders, there were those in the church and school who were truly Godly, loving, and helpful. I will never forget those who came alongside my older brother and me when our parents split up. Included is a picture of one of PC's best basketball players taking my brother, Jerry, and me to a game. There were others, including Sunday school teachers, youth directors, and men and women of the church, who also came to our rescue.

My brother and I with a PC
basketball player

What was I Thinking?

Freshman Year

It was 1964; I was seventeen, high school was over, the Southern California skies were blue, the weather was warm, the surf was up, the girls were beautiful, blond, sleek, and in short skirts. The Beatles were in, the Beach Boys were hot, Hollywood was minutes away, and I had chosen to attend a Nazarene College. Even as a Christian, what was I thinking?

Chapter 1

Registration Day (September 6, 1964)

PC's day of registration began early; I was in no hurry to arrive as I only lived about five miles from the school. When I got to campus, I immediately ran into my two old Nazarene church buddies, Kurt and Jake. For the past seven years, we had been inseparable. We attended the same schools, played on the same basketball teams, went to the same church, and almost on cue rededicated our lives to Christ every year on our annual youth mission trip to the Navajo Indian reservation in Arizona. We were like peas in the same pod.

Registration at PC did not warrant an early arrival. The school's enrollment was just barely above 1,100 students. That was small in comparison to our high school which enrolled over 4,000 students and was one of the largest schools in Southern California. High school graduation was so large that it had to take place at the Rose Bowl with another big high school in our town as there was no other facility large enough in Pasadena to take care of so many students.

As registration began most classes were available and hardly full, so we took our time surveying the ones we might want to take. As we did other students poured into the old gym that day, but

Kurt, Jake, and I were hardly concerned and simply *shot the bull*. Many of the new students were from little communities all around California, like Modesto, Porterville, and Yreka. PC and Southern California were a big deal to them but not to us. As we watched all the commotion, we caught sight of other familiar faces. The auditorium was huge because it was built to serve as the college gym, chapel, and a place to host the annual Summer Nazarene Camp meeting which was kind of an indoor big-tent evangelistic crusade. It was at these meetings each summer that we met the familiar faces we saw now. After a while, we got in line and got things going.

As we made our way to the freshmen orientation table, we recalled some of those camp meeting experiences. Camp meetings were no small affairs as usually 2,000 Nazarenes and their families gathered each August. There was preaching, singing, and a lot of hand waving. It was like a Pentecostal gathering without tongues. Kurt reminded Jake and me of the girls we used to *hawk down* (check out) during these meetings. Our goal was to take out the prettiest of the bunch and *make out*. Kurt usually won that contest. The only negative thing was that some of these girls felt guilty afterward and would end up confessing their secretive moments of kissing at the camp meeting. That could get a little embarrassing. They thought they had lost their salvation by *making out* and had to do something about it. It did not bother the preaching evangelist though, as he went away feeling good about all the young souls he had just won to the Lord.

As we got a little closer to the front of our registration line, Jake brought up one last camp meeting memory, the "shaking fat woman." When we were not busy checking out the girls, we attended these camp meetings which lasted for about two hours. It was hot, the fans were blowing, but the show went on and was unrivaled. The preacher would jump up and down on the stage lifting his hands and shout, "Whew!" to get things started! Several in the audience would then shout back, "Amen," "Jeeeeeesus," and "Glory!" The way they said it was funny because they would drag out each syllable. We used to imitate them all the time. Every year on the last night of the camp meeting, the same large woman would get up near the end of the sermon and start shaking. It was like clockwork, and we could hardly contain ourselves. You can imagine this did not make our parents or youth directors too happy. She would shake and shake and then start screaming, "I've been saved! I've been saved! I've been saved! I've been saved by the blood of the Lamb." She would then start running around the entire auditorium, shaking and yelling. It was quite something to see.

Kurt, Jake, and I started laughing as we recalled this story, which brought on frowns from some serious looking registration supervisors. After we received our freshman schedules and a copy of the school rules, we moved on to another table to secure dorm room assignments. Jake and Kurt immediately put in to room with each other. It seemed to me they were pretty set on not opening up to any new relationships, especially if there was a risk of rooming with anyone outside of the Nazarene faith. This was where Kurt, Jake, and I disagreed. During our years at Pasadena High School, I never hesitated to strike up relationships with others outside of our Nazarene church. When I did, Kurt and Jake were critical of me and even standoffish at times. However, we always mended our differences and restored those temporary breaches of friendship.

Rooming with a non-Nazarene was a real possibility because PC did not have an exclusive enrollment policy as it allowed students to enroll from other faiths. It also stealthily accepted those who had no faith at all, especially if they were athletic and could help the school's sports program or had the money to simply pay the tuition. When these *no-faith* students came, only then did PC's evangelistic policy kick in. You know, the policy that says, "Well, perhaps they will become Christians through the school's Nazarene influence." So in actuality, the PC student body was a mix of Nazarenes, non-Nazarenes and those who didn't believe at all.

I told Kurt and Jake to go ahead and room together. I would take potluck. They were not surprised. I drew a guy named Darwin who I used to compete against in sports. We were not close friends, but I decided to make a go of it.

As I moved through to the next line to get some extra classes, I slipped behind an old girlfriend, Barbara. Barbara was not like any of the other girls I dated and definitely not like some of the Nazarene girls who attended PC. You know, the kind who wears ugly rimmed glasses, dresses that hit the floor, and looks like a 50-year-old missionary in an 18-year-old body. A girl who would also rush to join the Preacherettes at school, a society of gals whose goal in life was to marry a Nazarene pastor or missionary. These girls were obviously unlike the surfer beauties I used to stare at every day in high school with their long flowing hair, suntanned skin, impeccable bodies, and short skirts. Barb looked more like a surfer girl than a Preacherette. She was also the daughter of a very powerful and influential leader in the Nazarene denomination, who probably helped me get into PC at the last minute.

I decided to go to PC about two days before school started. I was already registered at Pasadena City College (PCC) across town and was set to play basketball there. Had I followed the original plan, I might have ended up playing for a neighbor of mine, Jerry Tarkanian, who came to PCC a couple of years later. Too bad for me in this respect, because Jerry went on to become one of the most renown basketball coaches in the NCAA winning a National Championship at UNLV.

I think Barbara's dad recommended me for PC as he knew that I treated her with great respect when we dated in high school. Dating Barb was a bit of a challenge, however. She was very smart and an attractive girl, but very shy and nervous about the whole dating process. She was quite a D.L., which in the 60s meant *door-lover*. In other words, Barb kept her distance from me no matter how many dates we went on. Eventually, I dated other girls but always remained good friends with Barb.

As I began to talk with Barb in line, I told her that I was surprised to see her at PC. "Barb," I said, "you should be at UCLA, it fits you more." She just smiled back and asked why I was at PC. I told her my grades in high school did not afford me too many choices. She knew that but was just trying to make me feel good. That was Barb, always complimentary, encouraging, and full of good things to say.

Just before registration ended for the day, I made my way to the checkout table where I met three new guys, Kerry and Lance, both from Colorado, and Doyle from Central California. They were what I would call free spirits or "no-faith" guys, as the Nazarenes might have described them. We hit it off immediately. I told them about a great beach for surfing, and we were on our way. As we left the building together, I ran into an old youth director who had helped lead me through many rededication experiences during my high school years. He gave me the same wary look that Kurt and Jake were famous for when I hung around non-Christians, but his was a little sterner. I didn't care as I was already attending another church.

My new friends and I headed off to Newport Beach. There weren't many freeways to travel on back then, so it took us about two hours to get there. Starving, we stopped off at a hamburger place selling five hamburgers for a dollar. Each of us got five hamburgers and downed them immediately. That would kill me today. When we arrived at Newport, the waves were spectacular. In all my years of surfing, I had never seen anything like this. These were 25, 15, and 10 ft. waves – it was incredible. Lance, who was from Colorado, had never even been in the ocean. He turned to me and said, "Is this the way it really is when you go surfing?" He was awestruck by both the beauty of the beach and the pounding of the surf. Only about ten surfers were attempting to surf these waves. Hundreds were lined up along the shore just watching.

Doyle, the guy from Central California, said, "What do we do?"

Kerry, Lance's friend and roommate from Colorado, said nothing.

I shouted, "Let's go and try it. Just follow my lead. When a big wave comes, swim under it; don't try to grab it and ride it in. This is the Wedge, and these waves will not only take you for a horrendous ride, but they will also dump you on the sand. It is one thing to get dumped on the sand by an eight-foot wave; it's quite another to be dumped by a wave that is two stories high."

Out we swam. After 30 minutes, Kerry pulled out of the water exhausted. Lance had given up, and I wasn't sure where Doyle was. I made it out to the big waves, but they were beyond me. So I swam in as carefully as possible not wanting to be on the crest of any huge wave. As I walked to shore, I yelled out, "Where's Doyle?" No one knew. Suddenly, I looked down and saw an arm in the water. I grabbed for it, and it was Doyle. I pulled him out. He was okay. Praise God! We just watched the rest of the afternoon.

On the way back, we talked about why each of us had come to PC. Lance had come on a baseball scholarship; he had no interest what-so-ever in the Nazarene church or the Christian faith. Kerry was the son of a minister and was just glad to get away from being a pastor's son. He came on a basketball scholarship. Doyle did not have anything else to do, so he decided to give PC a shot for a year. When asked why I came to PC, I told them it was a last-minute decision for I thought it would be easier than going to Pasadena City College which required more credits to get through. They wanted to know what I thought about the Nazarene church. I thought for a minute and told them I wasn't really a Nazarene at heart, even though I had grown up as one. I was a Christian and believed in Christ. After I shared this with them, it got fairly quiet on the way back to campus. During which time, I began to mull over why I liked hanging out with these guys but felt a growing distance between myself and the Nazarene kids with whom I had grown up. I wondered even more why I never felt guilty about it.

Chapter 2

East Dorm

Destruction of East Dorm

East Dorm was the oldest dorm on the campus. It was rickety, smelly, and eventually torn down not many years after I graduated. It was the place where all freshmen were housed. One thing you could say about East Dorm, though, was that it somewhat symbolized the rebellious nature of my class in that it probably needed to be disassembled for the sake of the school. To explain, there was a tradition during the first week of school that the sophomore class had the right to haze all incoming freshmen. The sophomores, up until our freshman class came along, were regarded as the most free-spirited class PC had experienced in a long time. True to their reputation, they were determined to haze our class like no other. However, we were not a class to be bullied and were waiting enthusiastically for their antics and the eventual raid on our dorm.

One midnight the sophomores demanded we leave our rooms and be dunked in the fountain, with other hazing embarrassments to follow. Most of the freshmen in East Dorm, particularly those on the first floor, went along with this demand, but there was a group of us on the second floor that determined to fight back and not accept any hazing whatsoever. As an air horn sounded to start things off, eight of us crammed into my room. We pushed the dresser against the door making it very clear to the sophomores that we were not going to go along with their demands. In frustration and then anger, they focused on getting into our room. They threatened us verbally, including a few un-Nazarene expletives. I was a little concerned how this conflict would turn out as it quickly escalated when they saw our resolve. Kerry, my friend from Colorado, threw a few expletives of his own back at them, including words like "chicken ending with excrement." This, of course, enraged them all the more.

For an hour they took turns battering our door and yelling. We took turns in shifts holding the door. It was getting intense. At one point, one of their biggest sophomores was able to get his hand inside the door and began to push with all his might. Others joined him, and it looked like they were going to win. My roommate, Tom, who was on a track scholarship, took his shoe off and smashed this guy's hand as hard as he could against the edge of the door. This big sophomore fell back, and we secured the door once again. Kerry began yelling at them that we had Tom's claw hammer and would smash them with it if they kept up their assault, but they proceeded to batter until the bottom half of the door caved in. We quickly moved our dresser back in place which served us well. The dorm supervisors finally came and called everything off. As the sophomores left, we yelled at them, "You chickens. You can't even carry off a hazing!" You can imagine the relationship we had with those sophomores over the next few years.

From that point on, Tom picked up the nickname *The Claw* and everyone called him that for a long time.

Old Pop Webber, head of our dorm and retired minister, came up and said, "Boys, I thought I'd seen the worst class last year, but you have far surpassed them!" When he went back to his room, unbeknownst to him, Kerry had set up a firecracker that would go off at the bottom of his door the minute he opened it. When he went through the door, another firecracker was set to go off above his head. I am sure we validated Pop Webber's assessment of our class.

Our class went on to win many of the competitions in sports for the next few years. We even defeated a stunned group of seniors in the final flag football game of the year, winning the championship. During the course of the years to come, particularly after we were finished at PC, a few of those second-floor free spirits came to know Christ and served Him fervently, very much like the free spirits that night when East Dorm was raided by the sophomores. In my observation, the students on the first floor by and large contributed very little to the kingdom of God because they were too steeped in a religious system of rules, regulations, and outward appearance as defined by the Nazarene church.

It was pretty clear to me after starting Campus Crusade for Christ on our campus who was willing to take the risk of sharing their faith on the streets of Hollywood or on the campus of Pasadena City College. It was not those on the first floor.

Chapter 3

Chapel

Chapel was a very important part of PC. Students were required to attend chapel every morning, Monday-Friday at 10:30. We did have some significant people speak in chapel on occasion, including Viktor Frankl a survivor of and writer about the Holocaust, but for the most part, chapel included only older Nazarene pastors that seemed clueless how to relate to college students. If we didn't go to chapel, we could get kicked out of school. We were allowed just so many absences, and then received a warning or school expulsion from Mr. Meddleson, a dean of students nobody liked.

I am not sure how many people liked chapel the way it was, but I know the free spirits I hung out with hated it. You could sit next to anyone you wanted for the first week of school, but then a formal seating chart was put together based on where you had been sitting. It could not be changed after that until the second semester. Of course, Kerry, Lance, Doyle, Tuffy, a new friend from the second floor, and I all sat together. This was important as you will see. Each row sat 12 students. In addition to our five, there were another seven students that filled out our row. Since no one checked very carefully, we worked out a system where each of us only had to attend chapel one day a week to sign in for the others. We did this blatantly, bringing different colored pens and altering our signatures as the attendance sheet was passed down the aisle. On any given day if you looked down our row, it would be about half full, but the sheet would have 12 signatures. The other people in our row eventually caught on to what we were doing. Instead of reporting us, they copied us and signed for each other too. There were literally days when there were only two or three students in the row, and yet 12 names appeared on the attendance sheet.

My row

My approach to chapel was probably not from the Lord, but I was not thinking of Him. Instead, during this time I often laughed about what I was doing and was just glad to get out of chapel. God never hit me with any apparent consequences nor did He take away my salvation as the Nazarenes constantly harped on for every misdeed or wrong-doing. I never felt an inkling of guilt for missing chapel. It didn't deter me from claiming Christ as Lord nor keep me from sharing Him with others as opportunities arose. The Lord didn't appear to hold me accountable; I think because He was beginning to teach me what His grace was all about. His grace is full of forgiveness, compassion, and great patience.

Chapter 4

Term Paper

Tom, my roommate, better known as Claw, was a conscientious student. Unlike me, he did *everything* possible to get good grades. His math professor told students if they attended every class without fail, they would at least get a passing grade. Tom's math class started at 6:30 in the morning, so he set his alarm to go off 45 minutes before the class started, got himself ready, and was there every morning. . . except one. Evidently the night before one of his final classes, I inadvertently disconnected his alarm clock, causing him to miss the class. Tom was incredibly angry with me. However, praise the Lord, he passed the class anyway. Later, he told me he felt moved by the Spirit to seek out a new roommate for the next semester.

I had a very different approach to my classes. Every morning I would get up and go to English which was scheduled at 7:30. Mrs. Roberson was a wonderful English teacher and a very godly woman. She started every class by reading CS Lewis' *Screw Tape Letters*. My dorm room was actually only three minutes from the classroom, so with a 7:30 start time I set my alarm for 7:25. In five minutes I could put on jeans, my moccasins, and get there in a pajama shirt (which became my school shirt). I made it on time every morning. I knew very little at that time about English, and I think Mrs. Roberson knew that. She was a very forgiving teacher, and I believe she really liked me. The class project to be completed by the end of spring was a term paper, counting for most of your grade. The whole second semester of this class was dedicated to teaching the students how to write term papers. I hardly listened and had pretty much forgotten the due date on the paper. (I was not serious about my studies during this first year in college as I was having too much fun getting to know all the free spirits who had come to PC.)

One day as I was walking down the hall of my dorm, Tuffy, one of my classmates asked, "How are you doing on your term paper?" (Now this was Friday.)

I responded, "I'll get it done; when it is due?"

Tuffy snapped back, "Monday!"

I was in deep trouble. I asked Tuffy if I got it done by Sunday would he type it. It only had to be 10 pages long. He agreed to a fee. Now all I had to do was write it. I hurriedly went to the library, and the first book I found was about the life of a brown bear. I immediately started to copy that book word for word. It only came out to four pages. So, I went back to the library after Tuffy had typed those four pages and changed the introduction to *The Life of the Brown Bear and the Polar Bear*. Now it was just about ten pages. As Tuffy was typing it, his typewriter broke, and he had to borrow someone else's. He didn't have time to retype the whole thing, so the second part of the paper was in a completely different type than the first part of the paper. As he got to the end, the ribbon ran out. We had to borrow a third typewriter which had a completely different type than the first two.

Tuffy asked if I wanted him to type out the footnotes at the bottom of each page or at the end of the paper.

I replied, "What's a footnote?"

He explained that every fact that had been taken from a book had to be footnoted and checked for plagiarism.

I asked, "What's plagiarism?"

He grumbled, "When you copy everything word-for-word from a book."

I inquired, "Is that a bad thing?"

He exclaimed, "It is a thing that will flunk you on this paper!"

It was Sunday, and I couldn't get the books back, so I said, "Just make them up."

He grunted, "Make them up?"

I responded, "I think I remember she was only going to check every third paper to see if the footnotes are correct. Let's just hope for the best."

The next morning I turned in my paper with three different types, bogus footnotes, and totally plagiarized. Amazingly, I got a "C" on the paper. I wasn't one of those she checked. To add insult to injury, Jake, one of my old buddies that roomed with Kurt, worked very hard on his paper but messed up on just one footnote. He got a "D" as his paper was checked. WHO SAYS THERE'S NO GOD?!

Chapter 5

Basketball

Even though I did not receive a scholarship for playing basketball, I had high hopes of not only making the freshmen basketball team but eventually playing varsity. I was not a significant part of my high school team and not even on the team my senior year. Our high school basketball team was so good that we ended up in the 4A finals in Southern California. Twelve out of 17 players on the team got scholarships of some kind to different colleges, and two of the players went on to play professional basketball.

Having to practice and play against these players all the time made me a good player, just right for a small college like PC. A month before I graduated from high school, the coach who made our team so great saw me play in a spring league and afterward came to me and apologized, saying that he blew it by not having me as a part of his team my senior year. He thought I was a pretty good player, or at least he said as much.

With that kind of confidence, I stepped right in and started playing with the varsity players at PC. They were hardly a challenge compared to who I had been playing against in high school. My pride grew and grew and grew. I admitted to the Lord in my prayers that I really loved basketball more than anything else. During those months before basketball season opened, I wouldn't even play with most of the freshmen players. I would only play with the best of the varsity. The day right before basketball season opened, I was playing 3-on-3 with some of the varsity players when I turned my ankle so badly that it was actually at a 45-degree angle. It puffed up and turned yellow and produced the most incredible bruise I have ever had. I strained all the ligaments, if not tearing some of them. I tried coming back the next week when basketball season opened, but I could not turn to the right or the left. The guys I had prided myself on being better than took full advantage. Even the freshman coach was unsympathetic to my injury and not helpful or encouraging. My basketball season was over. I limped back to the dorm after that defeating day; I could hardly walk, yet I had tried to make opening practice. Welling up in my heart came an amazing declaration. "God, if I need to give up basketball for You, then that is what I will do." I was sincere. Over the next few months, I felt that was what God was asking me to do. As a result, I never played for PC, although I did enjoy playing against the varsity players in the off-season.

During the first-off season, I remember playing against several of the varsity players in a Friday afternoon pick-up game. After playing for an hour or so, the coach who had been so unsympathetic to me came on the court. He was with a couple of other varsity players and they were going to play against my team. When he entered the court, I realized I was still angry about his uncaring attitude. This was made evident to everyone during the game. As he was going in for a layup, without thinking, I fouled him so hard that he fell to the ground and had to be carried off the court. He was in traction for a week. I knew then it was a certainty I would never be asked to play basketball for PC, but I had already made that decision anyway.

Years later when I was attending graduate school, I was still playing. I even practiced against some of the varsity players at the University of Wyoming. One afternoon, their coach saw me playing against his starting guards and asked me about my experience in basketball. He then invited me to come out and join the team. Evidently, the guys he saw me playing with were his best players, and I had played well against them. Unfortunately, graduate students were not eligible to play, so I had to pass on his invitation. The University of Wyoming team went on to play in the NIT championship that year. Even though my confidence was bolstered as a basketball player, I am glad about my earlier decision to lay aside basketball. There were many things I did in its place that were so much better, especially with respect to the things I did for the Lord. I feel certain had I dedicated all of my time to basketball, most of those things would not have been accomplished.

The PC Gym

Backdoor to the old PC gym where so many pick-up games were played

Chapter 6

Patent Leather Shoes (Not kidding)

At PC there were all kinds of legalistic rules and regulations. You couldn't go to movie theatres (no matter what the movie was), there was no smoking, no drinking, no playing cards (rook was okay), and no foul language permitted. Guys were in guy dorms and girls in girl dorms. Curfew was 10:00 pm, Sunday through Thursday, and 11:00 pm on Friday and Saturday nights, even for seniors.

In regard to clothing, the rules were even stricter, particularly for girls. Now, I hate to say this, but some of the girls at PC were something not to behold. Did I say "not" to behold? To be fair, there were more than a few that were pretty; however, in my opinion, many looked and acted like they came out of the depression. I think they could have been pretty, but the way they dressed did not help them. This was because of PC's dress code.

Shorts were not allowed. This was even true for some of the men's basketball teams of the past who had to wear sweats to games. That was the case until the NCAA stepped in and mandated athletic shorts be worn or elimination from further competition. The cheerleaders had to keep their skirts two inches below the knee, which was a little different than the cheerleaders at my high school. It seemed to me that their skirts were no longer than two inches from their waist.

Girls were not allowed to wear tight sweaters, pants, or jeans, or tennis shoes during class hours. Dresses and skirts had to be below the knee.

I remember one Saturday evening in the cafeteria when I saw my good friend Donna wearing a full-length raincoat. I went over and sat by her, and said, "Donna, it is 80 degrees out and sunny. Why are you wearing a raincoat?"

Donna looked up at me exasperated and, with a roll of her eyes, said, "It was either the raincoat or no food."

"What do you mean?" I asked.

"Oh, Kent, I have been at the beach all day with friends and got back just in time for dinner. They told me I couldn't wear jeans in the dining room and there were only five minutes to grab some food. By the time I went to the dorm, changed clothes, and got back, it would have been too late. I was starving. I saw this raincoat that someone had left behind on the clothes rack, and I went into the bathroom, took off my jeans and then some because the raincoat was too tight. I put my clothes in the closet in the bathroom. They let me in for dinner with no problem."

"So, under that raincoat is not too much?"

"Not a whole lot, Kent."

"That's exciting."

"What's exciting is that I get to eat!"

The girls even had a particular shoe style recommended for campus: shiny patent leather. This backfired in one instance, because supposedly if certain patent leather shoes were shiny enough and the right color they fuzzily reflected a girl's underwear. I wasn't sure this was true, but it certainly got my attention when a bunch of my free-spirited friends told me about it one day. I had always wondered why some of them occasionally stood at the

My reflection in today's version of a patent leather

bottom of the stairs when the girls walked down after class. I was never tempted to look myself. One of the adjunct professors got wind of the rumor and in response gathered all the guys together in his class and rebuked them for passing around such a story. He said in closing, "Guys, if you've seen one girl without her underwear, you've seen them all, so move on and cool it."

He must have known because we found out later he was having an affair with one of the staff girls.

Chapter 7

Mr. Prebble

It was Christmas my freshman year, and I had a unique schedule with three weeks off. This allowed me to gain much-needed employment during vacation break. I was broke. Tuition was fairly high at $1,800 a year. Through a friend, I got wind of a job selling Christmas trees. PC had a good reputation in the community, and I think I was hired because I was from PC. The pay was decent at $1.50/hour, for eight hours a day.

It was fun selling Christmas trees. I would take the customers around the lot, they would pick a tree, and I would carry it to the cashier's stand for them. Although the owner, Mr. Prebble, was not on site, there were some very strict and clear rules that his employees had to follow: show up on time, work hard, and never accept any money for a tree. All money had to come into the cashier. This was to stop any employee from stealing. The tree lot business manager said that from time to time Mr. Prebble would come on the lot to see if we were following the rules. I really did not know what he looked like, but one night unbeknownst to me, he showed up on my shift.

He singled me out, and we walked around the lot. He picked a very expensive tree. He said, "Hey, I am in a hurry. Here is $30; just take the money up to the cashier so I can leave."

I said, "I can't do that. You are going to have to go up to the cashier, and I will be glad to carry the tree for you. I am not allowed to take any money for any tree, and I am not going to."

He pressed me further. "Look, I will give you a $10 tip. I have to get going, and I need this tree. Can't you just make an exception this time? What kind of an owner do you work for?"

I explained, "I am not sure. I have never met him, but I am going to follow his rules." He left in a huff.

Thirty minutes later when I was bringing up a tree for another customer, he was at the cashier's stand. "Do you know who I am?" he asked.

I said, "No."

The gentleman replied, "I am Mr. Prebble, and I own this lot and a few of the restaurants in this area. I want to commend you for your character." He then turned to the business manager and told him, "Give Kent all the hours he wants to work."

He turned back to me and said, "When you are finished with the Christmas tree lot, you can come to me anytime to any of my restaurants, and you have a job." The next Christmas I again worked for Mr. Prebble, and he made me night manager.

It amazes me today how honest I could be in this situation with Mr. Prebble and the opposite with something like chapel at PC. In my life getting a grasp on God's grace seemed to bounce from one extreme to the next. How could I be dishonest in the chapel, yet honest with this non-Christian? I believe that God saw me as a work in progress. He was in control, knew what He was doing, and understood where I was headed.

Chapter 8

Intramural Sports

Even though I couldn't play basketball at the school because of my ankle injury, I was able to play for our freshman intramural basketball team after I recovered. The intramural competition between the classes was pretty competitive, more so than other years. In the past, the seniors usually won first place in each sport, then the juniors, sophomores, and in last place were always the freshmen.

At the beginning of the school year, this proved true with football. The freshmen ended up dead last as expected. But, that started to change during the basketball season when we began defeating the other classes. Since basketball was the number one sport at our school, this made them increasingly antagonistic towards us. This included the sophomores who tried to intimidate and haze us at the beginning of the school year. I don't

I made the shot

think they ever got over their failed hazing attempts, especially since we enjoyed reminding them of it, repeatedly.

Nevertheless, our freshman team was pretty good, due to several guys having played basketball in high school. As the season progressed, we played each team twice, including the irritated sophomores. I probably did not help their attitudes, because after defeating them the first time around, I remember taunting them. Not too spiritual of me I would say.

In the second round, we did pretty well again and had our last game against the sophomores. However, there was a transfer student who had just come in who joined them. He was a guy who had been kicked out of PC the year before. His name was Ralph; he was very tall and quite competitive, even more so than me.

As this last game progressed, there was no shortage of elbows, fouls, or intimidation from both teams. In the fourth quarter, I was under the basket trying to protect a rebound when Ralph came over my back. I gave him an elbow to the face. Next, while dribbling down the court, I was purposefully tripped from behind. I fell to the floor, smashed my chin, and bled everywhere, thanks again to Ralph. I went to the sidelines and put ice on my chin to stop the bleeding. To add insult to injury, we lost the game.

Afterward, I needed someone to take me to the hospital to get stitched up. The last guy I expected to help me was Ralph, but he came over and offered to take me. Since "beggars can't be choosers," I accepted. We piled into his old corvette and off we went to St. Luke's.

While at the hospital getting stitches, Ralph began to share with me his past experiences at PC. As he spoke, I grew more and more disgusted at the school for the legalism and hypocrisy it exhibited to him. He angrily blurted out toward the end of our talk, "I can never believe in Christ because of what I have experienced." I was unfazed as I had come from a high school where non-belief and rejection of God were common. I merely listened and commented that I understood. I didn't really understand, but that is what I said. As we concluded the conversation, I shared my own personal relationship with Christ and left it at that. I think he was surprised that I did not judge or reject him for what he said.

Over the next few months, we became good friends. Because of this, Kurt and Jake and many of my other friends from the Nazarene church began to criticize me for spending too much time with Ralph. They said if I hung around him long enough, I would lose my faith and become just like him. I ignored them and continued to build a relationship with Ralph, along with many of the other free spirits on campus.

During the spring, I joined another Nazarene youth group because a guy named Sonny was the youth director. In my experience, as I look back, he was the best youth director in the Nazarene denomination. I joined his youth group in large part because he had an outstanding singing group that traveled all over California. I loved music. We sang, gave testimonies, and openly shared our lives with one another, but most of all, our relationship with the Lord grew. It was the best experience I ever had as a Nazarene. Even though there was the presence of legalism at the college, there were some very credible things about many Nazarenes that were good and honoring to the Lord.

On one of our trips during Easter break this year, we were scheduled to do a five-day singing tour in San Diego where Ralph's parents lived. I told Ralph I would be down there with the singing group. He was at home on spring break. He hemmed and hawed and said he really did not want to go to another Nazarene church even if I was there singing. I said, "That's okay, I will see you when I get back from Easter vacation."

On the last night of our tour, where once again we were at a Nazarene church, the songs we were singing and the testimonies we were giving had a tremendous impact on those attending. As we were finishing, I looked back, and in the last row, I saw Ralph. Of course, I connected up with him right afterward and asked, "How in the world did you ever track us down?"

He replied, "I called around to all the churches to see who was hosting your singing group."

I asked him, "Why?"

Ralph said, "I don't know why; I just wanted to be here. I have a few more questions I want to ask you, and I want to say that tonight, even in a Nazarene church, I was greatly impacted by the message of Christ."

We went to my car where we could have a private conversation. I do not remember the questions he asked, but I do remember that Ralph accepted Christ into his life at the end of the conversation. We immediately prayed, and Ralph walked into the kingdom of God and has been there ever since.

Chapter 9

Circle "K"

During the first weeks of school, there was an effort by the student leadership on campus, (mainly the juniors and seniors) to identify up-and-coming school leaders. It was not announced in any formal way, but there was a male-only leadership "club" on campus called the Circle "K." It was through Circle "K" that you became a designated student leader on campus. The Circle "K" on this campus appeared to not want any free spirits or geeks as members.

Neither my friends nor I were asked to join. We were not even interested, but we did want to knock this elitist group down a peg or two. They wore blue blazers on campus showing everybody they were PC's elite. In reaction, we ordered some night shirts from a Colorado University that were red and had a Circle "C" on them. When these guys would bunch together on campus in their blazers, we would bunch together in our shirts chanting, "Circle C, Circle C, Circle C." They were put off as you can imagine because they knew we were making fun of them.

Some of the Circle "K" members really began to hassle me because of this, but I was hardly fazed by their bravado. In fact, to bug them even more, I often wore a sweatshirt around them on campus with a big muscle-bound creature on the front and the words, "If you can read this you are too darn close" on the back. The shirt came from a popular TV series at the time called *The Hulk*. One day as I wore this sweatshirt to the applause of many of my friends in the Circle "C" club, one of the Circle "K" members came up from behind and yelled, "I am too darn close, so what are you going to do about it, McClain?" His name was Mike, and he was basically a good guy, but I guess I got to him. I laughed at Mike, told him he was lucky this time and walked away. He was not amused.

Later that afternoon, I went to the gym to play basketball as I often did in the spring on Friday afternoons. The competition was always pretty good, and there was a system where you entered the lower court, and if you won, then you moved to the upper court. I took Ralph with me and picked up my friend Tuffy who had saved my academic life by typing my *Brown Bear, Polar Bear* term paper. Mike was on the upper court with his team and seemed to be waiting eagerly to see if we won.

We did get to the top court, and Mike immediately yelled out, "I've got McClain." He played pretty rough, elbowing me several times during the game, yet to his frustration we continued to defeat his team. For the last basket, the ball came to me, and Mike was going to make sure I did not sink that shot. I had another agenda in mind after being hit so many times. I dipped my shoulder as if to shoot, causing Mike to jump up to block it, but as he came down, I purposely put my shoulder into his chin. Mike fell to the floor and was knocked cold for a few seconds. He had to be taken to the hospital to be stitched up. Afterward I didn't feel good about what I had done, and in fact, I felt rather guilty. Later, I apologized to Mike, and he ended up becoming a good friend.

I am not sure how everyone in that Circle "K" group turned out, some better than others I suspect. Nevertheless, I was glad to be the first, only, and last president of the Circle "C" club. With the exception of the one incident with Mike, I felt good about the message we brought. That message being when Christians start making themselves elite over others, they need to be brought down a notch. And that goes for Circle "K" members at a Christian college, elders, pastors, and Christian leaders of all kinds in churches and colleges. My way may not have been the best, but I feel to have done nothing would have been even worse.

"Circle C ...Circle C... Circle C"

Chapter 10

Noah's Ark

To finish off my freshman year, I end with a story my friend Ralph shared with me about an experience he had in East Dorm the year before I arrived. It's hilarious yet also shows his great distaste for living life by rules and regulations, even if they are Christian in nature. I have told this story so many times that I thought for a while I had actually participated in it, but I didn't. If I had, I would have been right on board with what Ralph did.

It was irritating in East Dorm to have four different groups of students living together on two floors which did not always get along. The students on the first floor, for the most part, were ideal Nazarenes, compliant in every way. Primarily, the students on the second floor consisted of pseudo-Nazarenes, non-practicing Nazarenes with Christian hearts, or simply non- believers. Ralph and I were a part of the third group of non-practicing Nazarenes with Christian hearts.

Bob was one of the guys on the first floor. He was so self-righteous that he often prayed as loud as he could at night asking God to keep him from becoming sinful like the others in the dorm. His prayer went something like this: "Oh, Lord, help me not to be like the others in the dorm. Help me to be without sin." He would pray this so loud that it could be heard in other rooms, particularly the one right above which was Ralph's. I am not sure what his goal was. Maybe, he hoped that others would listen and actually stop sinning?

Ralph ended up getting pretty sick of hearing this guy's prayer rants and decided to do something about it. He began by sticking a vacuum cleaner hose down the heater vent to Bob's room while he was away at classes. The hose became a homemade intercom. The next night a bunch of guys on the second floor gathered in Ralph's room. When Bob started his prayer, "Oh Lord, I thank Thee that I am not like the other sinners in this dorm," Ralph lowered his voice and spoke loudly into the vacuum hose, "Bob!" Everyone in Ralph's room remained quiet waiting to hear how Bob would respond. When he didn't, Ralph tried again, "Bob!" Still, there was silence. A third time Ralph said, "Bob, this is the Lord!" More silence! Everyone in the room could hardly contain themselves. On his fourth attempt, Ralph yelled even louder, "Bob, this is the Lord!"

At which time Bob replied, "Yes, Lord, yes!"

Ralph then spoke out, "Bob, go build an ark." At this point, everyone busted loose laughing. According to Ralph, Bob got the message and never prayed that way again. This is certainly one way to dissuade self-righteousness in others.

Chapter 11

Summer of 1965

At the end of the school year, one of my old Nazarene buddies, Rick, arrived back home from Nampa Nazarene College in Idaho. He grew up only a block away from the PC campus but wanted a different college experience. Rick's mom called to see if I would like to join her when Rick showed up. I did, and for the longest time that day we reminisced about some of our old adventures at church and in high school.

One of those adventures was our Easter vacation trips to the Navajo and Hopi Indian reservations. These trips not only had a good impact on the Indians to whom we were ministering but on us as well. Usually, on Palm Sunday weekend, we arrived at Bresee Nazarene Church with sleeping bags and suitcases and got on a bus with 40 other high school and college students. As we ministered to the Indians for a week, we would visit their Hogan dwellings and sing and share our testimonies with them. Then we would invite them to an Easter service at the end of the week where we did more of the same.

Of course, during this trip, many of us received Christ again or rededicated our lives to Him. Rededicating our lives was not a bad thing, in fact, in most cases, it was good. However, to be saved and resaved over and over again, as the Nazarenes encouraged, was not helpful to develop a mature walk with God. Typical Nazarenes in those days did not go out into the world and present the Gospel to others because they were consumed with getting re-saved over and over again. As I learned later, it is an impossible burden to maintain your own salvation instead of letting God do this as He promised. This aside, these trips were fantastic experiences and served as lasting memories for most of us.

On the way back home from our trip, we always stopped by Hoover Dam where we would get out and have a contest to see who could throw the Frisbee the farthest over the dam. While doing this one year, the assistant youth director uttered a supposed profanity. At least that was what we thought we heard. We turned our heads when he said, "Would you please get back to the damn parking lot where the bus is!" Well, it was the "dam" parking lot he was referring to, not the "damn" parking lot as we thought. The two words sound exactly the same, and for the rest of the afternoon, some of us made up our own phrases to shock others, including the dam lights, the dam road, and the dam bathroom. Our humor was liberating to tell you the truth, a freedom we did not always experience as Nazarenes.

When Rick and I returned home, our spirituality seemed to have faded somewhat. We decided to play one of the funniest, yet most callous tricks on a friend in our group. Rod was always bragging about how hot he was on dates with girls. This was hard for us to believe, knowing him as we did. Anyway, we decided to find out for ourselves just how hot he was. We knew he had a date on Friday night, so we decided to join him without his knowledge. Rick and I hid in the backseat of his big car with a blanket over us. We weren't sure it would work but decided to go for it. We could hardly restrain ourselves as Rod first stopped at a gas station, fueling up, washing his windshield, and rehearsing what he was going to say to his date. He sang, "Saturday Night, Saturday Night," and at the same time practicing in a low voice, "Baby, this is big Rod here to pick you up." I don't know how we held ourselves together. He picked her up, and she sat right next to him. Off we all went. Rick got inspired as Rod was driving and put his hand on the girl's shoulder from the back. She thought it was Rod's hand. However, when she looked over and saw it wasn't, she screamed. Rod looked back and saw us. He immediately stopped the car and told us to get out. We had to hitchhike home. I don't think we ever saw anyone as surprised and embarrassed at the same time. Rod later forgave us and even joined in with sharing the story with others.

That is the way it was in high school as Rick and I recollected, in one instance serving the Lord and in another quite the opposite. I don't think God was ever uptight with me for my inconsistency, for He knew where I was going and how I would end up. Too bad more Nazarenes didn't have His grace perspective.

As Rick and I ended our conversation, I had to take off quickly, for I was late to a summer school class I had enrolled in at PC. It was about the life of John Wesley who was one of the spiritual heroes in the Nazarene Movement. Although Wesley was touted as a great evangelist and preacher in his day, I was not greatly impressed with him. As I read about his life in one textbook, he seemed legalistic, tight, and self-righteous. In fact, in his first ministry in America, he was asked to leave because of his legalism. On the way back to England in defeat, Wesley questioned his own salvation. Eventually, he did make a commitment to Christ and did some good things for the kingdom, but his works were always heavily laced with rules, regulations, and methods. Sound familiar?

While going to summer school, I also had a great job working at the Boys Club. One of the guys with whom I worked named BJ also went to PC. BJ was older and a little different than most. In school, for instance, he got through each class by cheating, even bragging about it. He got through to his junior year before the pressure of doing this got to him, and he quit.

On the weekends after work, BJ and I usually cruised in his '64 black two-door station wagon. We would play Beach Boys music and go from one Bob's Big Boy drive-in to the next. There were seven in the Los Angeles City area at the time. It was the thing to do in the 60s, especially if you had a hot car like BJ's. To draw even more attention when we cruised, we would take his 180 pound St. Bernard with us. The dog would sit in the front passenger seat which drew a lot of looks and laughs. We thought we were cool!

The summer finally ended, and it had been a good one, time to go back to PC for my second year.

Kent McClain

Sophomore Year

Old Music Building at PC

Chapter 12

Simonized

Right before school started in September, Ralph and I developed one of our most important relationships with a guy named Kyle. He had just finished medical school at USC, but he decided to work on a Master's in Biblical Studies at PC before beginning his residency.

I met Kyle at church and was immediately impressed with him. I was surprised that he would take time out in the middle of his preparation to become a medical professional to work on such a degree. He shared with me the theme of his thesis that he was just finishing, *Jesus the Servant* from the Gospel of Mark. I introduced Ralph to Kyle, and that triggered several conversations between the three of us about the life of Christ.

During this time, Kyle was very committed to taking groups of young boys on campouts for the purpose of sharing Christ with them. He asked Ralph and me if we would like to join him and 12 boys on a trip to Yosemite. I had heard Yosemite was beautiful, but I had never been there. Ralph and I couldn't join Kyle and the boys for the first part of the trip, but we were able to get there for the latter half.

When Ralph and I traveled to Yosemite to join up with the group, we took the old Manzanita Road. At one point Ralph asked, "Do you know where you are going?"

I said, "Why? I looked it up on the map."

"Did the map indicate it was a dirt road? Because that is what we are on right now."

"It is too late to do anything about it now," I replied. "So we will see if we get there or not."

After driving another 25 miles on dirt, we hit pavement again, and then an entrance to Yosemite appeared. We were relieved as it was pitch dark.

We worked our way down to the group campground and arrived about 1:00 in the morning. Kyle met us and said, "Throw your bags down anywhere. You look beat."

Ralph replied, "Anyone would look beat after driving with Kent for eight hours."

Kyle mentioned, "Before you go to sleep, throw all your food in the trunk of your car otherwise bears will come and take it."

We did and fell fast asleep. In the morning we woke up to see El Capitan a magnificent sheer rock wall that took my breath away and was one of the most awesome sights I had ever seen. I fell in love with Yosemite.

As we were eating breakfast with Kyle and the boys, a bunch of rough looking guys drove into the campground. After looking around to see where they were going to camp, they said that they had reservations for the spot where we had set up camp. Kyle said, "There are 20 empty spots in this campground, and we are the only two groups here. You want us to move?"

They replied, "Yes, so move your stuff!"

So we took our tents down, packed up our food, and moved our cars to another campsite. Later on that evening after eating dinner with the kids and having devotions, we packed up our food and put it in the trunk. I asked Kyle, "Is this really necessary?"

He said, "Oh, yeah. Bears have a reputation for breaking into campsites and ripping up food chests and tents."

As we looked across at the other group of campers, we noticed all their food was left in the chests on top of the picnic tables. Kyle whispered, "Shall we tell them about the bears?"

Ralph replied, "They should have gotten that from the park rangers when they came in."

"Kent, what do you think?" Kyle wanted to know.

I joked, "Isn't there a teaching in Scripture that says 'reap what you sow'? I think we should let this Scripture play out with these guys. Who knows, maybe this bear thing is an exaggeration." So we went to sleep, and they went to sleep.

In the middle of the night, there was a huge commotion going on near the other campers' tents. The next morning, sure enough, the bears had come in and ripped apart every one of their food chests. There was not one morsel of food left. Then I said, "There you go. You reap what you sow."

Ralph replied sarcastically, "You are so spiritual."

It is funny that I was excited to share the truth of the Gospel with the kids but not willing to share the truth of the bears with the other campers.

During the rest of the trip, we listened intently every morning to Kyle's teaching on what he called "The Servant Mission." Kyle was a brilliant teacher; he was not like any Nazarene I had ever met. Ralph and I had a great time with the boys on this trip, and we were even able to witness to them. More than anything, for the first time, Ralph and I began to understand what the Christian life was all about with respect to God's love, grace, and forgiveness.

This eventually led us to start a Bible study on campus, which we called the Markan's study. Ralph and I gathered about 15 students and had Kyle teach us what he had learned about Jesus being a servant according to the book of Mark. I'm not sure how others were impacted by the study, but I certainly was. Because of it, I did not try to get out of chapel this semester as I had done the year before.

On top of this, I even responded in one of the chapels to a call to be sanctified. The Nazarene view of sanctification is that if you really never want to sin again, all you need is to be sanctified. You do this by simply going to the altar after the service is over and surrendering yourself never to sin again. Feeling very spiritual that day in chapel after the chaplain issued the call, I went down and got sanctified. Afterward, I felt pretty good. For that entire day, in my own mind, I did not sin. I said kind words to others. I thought good thoughts. I even went around the campus picking up trash. Because of their respect for me, my free-spirited friends were not critical of my commitment. They slipped into the shadows hoping I would change my mind. Fortunately for them, the next day I sinned. For the first time, I began to realize that sanctification, which is growing in Christ, was a process, not a one-time decision. Over the years I would learn that I could never be sinless, but if I trusted God, I could sin less.

Apart from what I was learning, chapel continued as usual, teaching students they were sinners and either needed to be saved, resaved, or sanctified. Because of such poor teaching, many students ended up feeling guilty all of the time and regularly went forward to the altar to be resaved or re-sanctified. Thus many students became ashamed of their walk with God and confessed just about everything under the sun just to stay saved or sanctified. They were even confessing things that were just thoughts, temptations, or behaviors that weren't sins at all.

One day a guy came up to the altar and confessed that he had slept with his girlfriend. Imagine how she must have felt when he did this. As it turned out, he had actually fallen asleep on his date with her, as he had worked all day and was tired. He had done nothing wrong. It just shows how ignorant he was about sex. That was not true of some Nazarenes I knew; they would not drink, smoke, go to shows, or play cards but would have plenty of sex.

After a few weeks, I felt I had to make my point about sanctification, and of course, I was back to being my mischievous self again. Following chapel one day, I told a guy who had just been sanctified that he also needed to be simonized. "Simonized?" he asked, "What is that?"

As Ralph and some of the curious free spirits listened in, I explained, "It is a third work you need to do to be completely cleansed of all sin." (I got the term simonized from the car wax I used on my 63 Valiant. You could give your car a brilliant shine and lasting protection according to the label. It was kind of a sanctifying approach to cleaning your car.) To my surprise, he believed me. Of course, my only point of this was to show how faulty a one-time commitment to sanctification was. I ended by telling him to be simonized was a double dose of sanctification and then told him just to ask one of the spiritual leaders who was in charge of chapels. He did, and I was in big trouble with the school for quite some time after that.

Reflecting back, I should have just told him what sanctification was rather than make fun of it and confusing him. Needless to say, again, I was still a work in process with the Lord, a mixture of His grace and my ever-present flesh.

Chapter 13

Betas

PC was a small college and had only three or four major sports in which they competed with other colleges. Some students came to PC with fairly decent athletic backgrounds. Several had been good players on their high school teams. Therefore, in addition to playing for the school, some athletes also participated in the intramural sports program when their season was over.

At the beginning of my sophomore year, the intramural program was gutted and revised. For years it had pitted the freshman class against the sophomores, juniors, and seniors. Supposedly, the longer you were at PC, the savvier you became in winning these competitions. Therefore, the seniors usually won. The only exception was my freshman class and the sophomore class the year before. *Higher-ups* decided to change the program so the students would be split up into four athletic groups with a mixture of freshmen, sophomores, juniors, and seniors in each. The four groups were the Alphas, Betas, Gammas, and Deltas. I had the fortunate experience of landing with the Betas who ended up winning many of competitions that first year. My friend Kerry was a Beta as well. He was basically a good guy but struggled mightily with Christianity. Evidently, his dad, who was a Nazarene pastor, put a lot of pressure on him to be a model Christian and Nazarene. It had the reverse effect on him. Sad to say, this was a common mistake many Nazarenes made with their kids. They drove Christianity down their throats with strict spiritual expectations, rules, and regulations.

As a result, Kerry ended up hardly a Christian at all and was coarse at times in what he said and did. For example, after we had won the football championship, he proudly announced at the victory party that we were all truly the best *masterbetas* ever. Many of the guys really started to laugh. I didn't; I didn't know what was so funny. I was totally unaware at the time of what masturbate meant which was probably a result of my own Nazarene upbringing. I eventually found out, and now looking back, it was pretty funny. Sadly, Kerry continued down a path like too many others at PC and did not exhibit much of a Christian life. I am not sure how he and those like him turned out, but the stories I've heard over the years have not been encouraging

Beta Championship football team? Possible!

Chapter 14

The Lonely-Heart Spinster

Reflecting on the Nazarene take on sanctification, I realized there was a great deficiency in their practice of the Christian life when it came to God's grace. Once again, I returned to my own application of the Christian walk where at one moment I proclaimed Jesus as Lord to others, but in the next moment, I enjoyed rebelling against and playing pranks on the Nazarene establishment. I could embrace Christ, for He was full of grace and truth, but I couldn't accept the Nazarene view that was weak in God's grace. As a result, my former attitude towards chapel returned; that is, I tried to get out of everyone possible.

When the spring quarter began, the seating chart for chapel was passed around and established. You could sit anywhere you wanted, with whomever you wanted, but you had to stay put. As I took my seat assignment next to Donna, a good friend of mine, I got an inspired idea of how to get out of chapel. I knew that one of the persons working with chapel attendance was a woman who was a 40-year-old spinster. She never married, didn't even date as far as anyone knew. To replace this missing part of her life, she immersed herself in the romantic gossip on campus. She delighted in it so much that I think it influenced some of her decision-making. I knew this because everyone talked and joked about it when there was nothing else to talk about.

As I took my seat next to Donna that first week, I told her I would probably not be there too much. I told her this because I did not want Donna to think it had anything to do with her. Donna was great about it and comfortable to talk with and be around. I probably learned more about girls from Donna and her friends Jennifer and Glenda than from anyone at that point in my life. They told me how girls think, what their emotions are like, and most importantly, what does and doesn't turn them on.

I missed one chapel after the next and was called in at the end of the year to account for my absences. On my way to Miss Anstin's office, the lonely-heart spinster, I asked Donna to accompany me. I had thought about this plan from the beginning, but now was the time to put it to work. This was yet another situation in my life where my understanding of grace did not always match with what Scripture actually taught. In my defense, I had a knack for saying things that were not actual lies but could easily be misinterpreted in my favor.

I brought Donna (who knew nothing of what I was doing) to Miss Anstin's office and asked her to wait outside. When Miss Anstin opened the door, I made sure that she could see that Donna was with me.

Miss Anstin hesitated as she looked out and saw Donna, and then she said, "Hi, Kent. I didn't know you and Donna were an item."

I hedged, "Well, kind of, it's been a little up and down with us. You know, friends one moment and then...." I purposely did not finish the sentence for I did not want to lie. Mislead, yes, but not an out-and-out lie. I could see on Miss Anstin's face the beginning of a tear.

She asked softly, "When did you break up?"

"Well, I would not say we broke up. However, she is here with me now, so isn't that a good thing?" At which time another tear trickled down her cheek.

Then Miss Anstin shifted the conversation back to my absences and said, "How do you account for all of these?"

I responded, "Well, Miss Anstin, Donna and I were sitting together in chapel at the beginning of the semester, and it became evident as our relationship swayed that I needed to sit elsewhere. At least, that was part of the reason I moved." (The other reason which I did not share with Miss Anstin was I just did not want to go to chapel.) I continued, saying to Miss Anstin, "I went to the back of the auditorium and began helping those taking chapel attendance. They were glad to have my help." (And that is really what I did, except that when we finished taking attendance which only took about 5-10 minutes, I took off for the Connal's Grinder down the street to have a donut and coffee. Kids in the 60s weren't into health foods like herbal tea and granola bars.)  "Miss Anstin, I did not miss a chapel, and Donna and I are on speaking terms, which really we have always been, just different speaking terms if you know what I mean."

Miss Anstin then exclaimed, "Well, I am thrilled you and Donna are back together, and as far as those absences are concerned, I'll take care of them. And if there is anything I can do to help your relationship with Donna, just let me know." Looking back, it is certainly a credit to Miss Anstin that she was willing to bend the rules because she was so trusting.

I said, "You have already done enough by being so understanding with my absences, but I will take your offer to heart."

As I walked out, Miss Anstin made a point to wink at Donna as we left together. I grabbed Donna's arm as we made our exit, which I had not really ever done before as we were just friends. Of course, Donna wanted to know what everything was all about and why I had grabbed her arm on the way out. When I told her the full story, she looked at me and said, "Kent, I can't believe you did that!"

Donna and I became closer and closer as friends. One night after one of our study sessions together, Donna and I talked about our relationship. We climbed to the top of the music building where most of the couples usually went to make out. We didn't do that but just sat looking down at the campus instead. Then, we talked for a while and came to the conclusion that we were just friends. After the school year ended, I did not see Donna again although we recently began communicating through email. She transferred to Nampa Nazarene College in Idaho, where she finished her schooling. Donna and I are still friends today after forty years, and amazingly, her son and my son are both on the mission field in different parts of the world.

Jennifer and Donna

Chapter 15

Follies-Bergere

During my sophomore year, I was just getting to know my new step-father, Don. My mother had remarried when I was a senior in high school. In an effort to grow our relationship, Don planned a trip for my mother and me to Las Vegas. My family really never had much money while I was growing up, so there weren't special trips like this. I was excited to be able to fly to Las Vegas, stay in a luxury hotel, have an expensive dinner, and even go out to a special show.

Before we went to dinner the first night, I went to the health club. Following a good workout and time in the whirlpool, I went into the sauna. After a few minutes, a familiar sports figure came in and sat down across from me. It took a while to figure out who he was. But finally, I asked, "Aren't you Sonny Liston who fought Muhammad Ali last year?"

He responded rather curtly, "Yes, I'm Sonny Liston." He really did not say much more after that, and I thought as I sat there that he was not nearly as big as he appeared on TV. I think he was about 6'1" and 218 lbs. at the time, but he was very muscular. But then, I had a good friend with whom I played basketball named Ray who was also 6'1," weighed 250 pounds, and had a 36-inch waist.

What was I Thinking?

Now he was imposing. I left the sauna and said on the way out, "Good luck." He didn't respond and, from what I understand, ended up dying three years later in a very mysterious way. A few years after this chance meeting, I would meet and talk with the guy who defeated Liston in the ring, Mohammed Ali. He pretty much dominated our conversation with his belief in Islam and the prophet Mohammed. He was nice, though, and gave me his autograph as a thank-you for talking with him.

Soon after leaving the sauna and returning to my room, Don called and said that it was time for dinner. I was excited for I knew this meal would be something special. When I arrived at his and my mother's room, we walked down and grabbed a cab, then off to the Tropicana. The show that night, the Folies Bergere, was perhaps a little risqué even for me, a rebellious Nazarene. There was an extent of nakedness throughout the show that surprised me, but I became less opposed to it as the show went on. Even the programs they gave to us were pretty spicy with lots of pictures of scantily clad girls. I did not throw it away.

Then as we were ordering, Don said to the waitress, "Give this young man a Rob Roy."

The waitress questioned, "Is he old enough?"

Don put a hefty tip on the tray and said, "If I say he is old enough, he is old enough."

The waitress brought me a Rob Roy. It was the first alcoholic drink I had ever had. When I drank it, something really surprising happened to me. All the sin and loss of salvation (drilled into me) I was supposed to feel after taking a drink did not come about. In fact, none of my feelings toward God changed, nor had His feelings toward me as far as I could tell. I mused over this during the rest of our trip and began to ask myself later on, what else have I been told that is not true?

We had a great evening and flew back to LA the next day. I called Kerry and showed him my Folies Bergere Program which he was very excited to see and borrowed for the next couple of months. I then called Ralph and told him I had taken my first drink.

"So what was it like?" he asked. "How did you feel?"

"Well, I'm still a Christian and haven't lost my salvation. Some of these Nazarene beliefs, Ralph, what are they thinking? Where does it say any of this stuff in the Bible?"

It was too bad that such a poor application of the Scriptures was taught to Nazarene young people, whether at school or at church. In the years to come, many left the church when they found out how shallow and inaccurate Nazarene teaching and applications were. Such doctrines even drove some of them to eventually opt for atheism rather than believe in God any longer. I discovered this talking at length with disillusioned former Nazarenes over the last couple of years.

In a final note, my step-father and I became good friends. I found him to be very wise and kind, and I enjoyed our conversations about spiritual subjects.

Chapter 16

The Post Office

The first semester of this second year ended three weeks before Christmas. PC did this intentionally so students could work a full month between semesters. It was very helpful because PC students were available for work far ahead of students from other schools coming home for Christmas. The best job was delivering packages for the post office during the holidays. In addition to being a night manager at Mr. Prebble's Christmas tree lot, I also applied to the US Post Office to deliver packages during the day.

The post office had a unique way of offering jobs to students. We had to bid on the job, and the lowest bidders got the jobs. Therefore, I would have to figure out how much it would cost me to use my car and what my time would be worth at an hourly rate. I got some good input on this from my first roommate, The Claw, who had done this before. I put in my bid.

Previous to making this bid, I met another fellow student at PC named Wendell. I first met him through a singing group at LA First Nazarene. He was the pastor's son; even so, I was still impressed with him. He was not only a good musician and pleasant to be around, but seemingly intelligent, too. Later, that would pay off for me big time.

Two days before putting in my bid, Wendell cornered me on campus and asked me how to make a decent bid because he also wanted to work for the post office. I told him, and we both got our bids accepted and started working.

Before I started this job, I was given more useful advice by Tom, the Claw. He told me to take my time delivering packages my first day as however many packages I could deliver that day would determine how many packages they would give me every day thereafter. With the post office, there were just so many packages they would allow you to deliver. If that number was 300 packages and it took you two days to deliver them, then you got paid just for two days of work. If it took you three weeks to deliver 300 packages, then they would be obligated to pay you for three weeks of work.

Because of Tom's input, I took only 15 packages with me on the first shift, and it took me about two hours to deliver them. Upon completion of those deliveries, I went back to the dorm, took a nap, then went down to the gym and played basketball for a couple of hours. After a late lunch, I then returned for my second shift of the day. Thus I had established that I could deliver about 30 packages a day. I don't know how this all worked into the grace of God, but I sure got paid a lot.

The Nazarene students whose lives were run by rules and regulations worked two or three days and found themselves having to find other Christmas jobs. My life was not run by a lot of rules and regulations, but by a steady, yet inconsistent and flawed, application of God's grace. Anyway, I shared my delivery approach with Wendell, who was reluctant to try it at first. In the end, he gave it a shot, and sure enough, it worked for him, too.

Wendell and I got together for several late lunches and did a lot of joking and getting to know each other during these times. Because of our time with each other, we decided to room together the next fall. Wendell helped me greatly academically, and I helped him to begin to take a lighter view of the Nazarene legalism he experienced over the years. Wendell and I are still close friends to this day, more than 45 years later. We still speak of our time at PC. Overall, it was worth every minute we were there.

Chapter 17

Balboa Week

During Easter vacation of this year, the Something Singers, a singing group I was a part of, was asked by Campus Crusade for Christ to be their opening act at the Balboa Pavilion. Also performing would be Andre Cole, a well-known magician. Campus Crusade's plan was to draw in as many students to the Pavilion as possible each evening for the purpose of sharing the Gospel. They felt that a contemporary singing group like ours could break the ice with many of the college and high school students invited to come to the Pavilion. So every night, our singing group opened up the Campus Crusade show. At the end of the show, a guy named Linus Morris, who was in charge, had one of his Crusade people give a dramatic testimony and he concluded with a message on how to be saved. At the end of the week, Linus came to us and asked if one of the singers or musicians in our group could give a testimony on the last night. Our leader Sonny immediately turned to me and said, "Kent will do it. He will give his testimony."

During the next few days, I thought a lot about what kind of a testimony I would give. Ralph came up to me and probed, "So what are you going say?"

I hesitated, "Ralph, I don't know. My story is so dull I doubt anyone would be interested."

Ralph then asked me to tell him my testimony.

"Well, I was six years old in my dad's church in Pasadena, California, and he issued a salvation call to come to the church altar if I wanted to be saved, and I went and got saved."

My dad asked, "Are you sure you know what you are doing?"

I said, "Yes" and then he prayed with me.

Ralph replied, "Yeah, that is pretty dull. Can you make up something?"

"I don't know, Ralph. I don't think I should be making up stuff when it comes to testimonies."

"Then," said Ralph, "I'll pray for you and God help you."

I responded rather sheepishly (and with a big gulp), "Thanks!"

While I prepared over the next couple of days, I was being discipled by one of Crusade's leaders who was about to be sent to Vietnam. I can't remember his name and don't know if he lived through the conflict, but he taught me how to step forward and share my faith with others no matter the circumstance. He showed me firsthand how to start up a conversation with someone about Christ and then lead them to salvation. He used Crusade's Four Spiritual Laws booklet to do this. It basically says, "God loves you and has a wonderful plan and purpose for your life. However, you cannot know or experience that plan or purpose because you are sinful and separated from God. But do not despair, for Jesus, His Son, was sent to be that bridge to God. All you need do is repent of your sins and ask Jesus into your heart. When you do this, you will be on the other side of that bridge with God, who will then begin to reveal His plan and purpose for you."

Pretty simple, yet very complete and filled with truth. After this Campus Crusade leader counseled and trained me, we then went and shared these truths with the first three guys we met one day on the beach. I will never forget their response. All three said "Yes" and prayed to receive Christ, right there on the beach in front of everyone. Can you believe that? Needless to say, I was taken back but thrilled at the same time. It showed me then and there that with God anything was possible; all I need do is step forth in faith.

When Saturday night came, not only had I found the time to pray and think about what I was going to say; I also had the faith and courage to go with it. The moment of truth finally arrived. The performances of Andre Cole and our singing group concluded, and the Pavilion was packed as it had been every night that week. Dramatic testimonies throughout the week had been very effective; many had come to Christ. When Linus brought me forward after our concluding song, it was my turn now. As I was about to speak, I could see Ralph at the very back of the auditorium holding his hands over his eyes.

I began by saying, "I don't know if many of you know this, but a few years ago I was in the Hell's Angels. One night as I was riding my Harley down Newport Boulevard during an intense rainstorm, I lost control of my bike. I slid all the way through the intersection and right into the front door of a small little church. As I skidded down the aisle, the preacher was giving an altar call. I raised my hand and said, "I believe."

The college crowd was not laughing as I thought they would but appeared a little spellbound and in awe. Then I continued, "That sounds like a very dramatic testimony, does it not? But to be honest with you, I really came to know Christ when I was six years old at the altar of my dad's church. Hopefully, you can see that you don't have to have a dramatic testimony to come into the kingdom of God. All you need to do is to put your faith in Christ whether on a motorcycle, at the altar of a church, on Newport Beach, or in the quiet of your own heart somewhere else."

Linus then came to the podium and gave a great concluding message, and many came to know Christ that night. To my surprise, several people came up to me afterward and asked if I was hurt during the motorcycle accident. There were even kids in my own singing group that said, "I didn't know you were a Hell's Angel." I don't think they heard my whole story, particularly the ending. Nevertheless, I told the truth and did not make anything up when all was said and done. Soon after, Ralph came up smiling and said, "Kent, you've got guts."

Later that summer, Ralph would have his opportunity to have his own guts, or faith, as I would frame it. While at Santa Cruz Beach, there was a big fight with spectators cheering on one fighter over the other. In the middle of the fight, Ralph stepped in between the two and said, "Have you guys heard of the Four Spiritual Laws?"

One of the guys, who evidently really did not want to fight, said, "No, what are they?"

Ralph then shared them with this guy and all those who stuck around. Now that is guts!

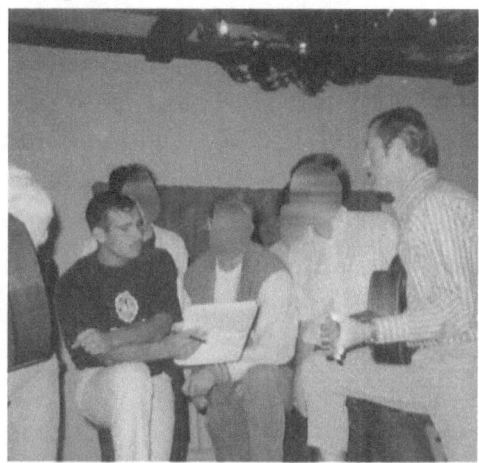

A few years later at the UCLA Jesus Christ Light and Power House, and still being discipled by Linus

Chapter 18

Hollygrove

As my sophomore year was drawing to a close, I wondered what kind of summer God had planned for me. I went into the placement office at school and looked at summer jobs because I was completely broke and needed money for the fall. The gal in the placement office said, "This might interest you, Kent since you like working with kids. It is advertised as a recreation director for Hollygrove Home for Children." I learned later it was an orphanage in Hollywood not far from Sunset and Vine. I thought to myself, "Wow, now that's cool working in Hollywood."

I immediately called and got an interview with the executive director, Eleanor, and her two assistants, Margaret and Bob. Since I had a fairly good year spiritually, I thought that whatever questions they asked me I would answer with complete transparency. I was not going to try to manipulate any answers just to get the job. I was beginning to see that even though God's grace forgave me no matter what I did, it should never be taken advantage of as I sometimes had.

Hollygrove was a two-story building on about five acres with a number of cottages where the kids lived. I was impressed. In addition to the cottages, there was a swimming pool, a nursing station, and a huge recreation field. All of the children had either been orphaned or taken away from abusive or neglectful parents. There were about 70 children in all on the premises.

I came in and sat down for my interview before the panel of three directors, and they began asking me about my experience working with children. I had some good experience, especially working for the Boys' Club the summer before. Then they asked me some more personal questions, about how would I feel about working with children who had been abandoned or abused? I told them I would be thrilled with the opportunity and even thought God had given me certain abilities with children. When I said "God," I could tell I had hit a button with all of them. As I looked at their surprised reactions, I said to myself, "Well, so much for that job."

Immediately, Margaret, the older of the three, said, "What do you mean by God giving you the ability to work with children?"

I shared with her and the others about what I had done during the last year at school.

The executive director quickly inquired, "Well, are you going to share Christ with these kids too?"

And Bob joined in, "Do you know we are not a Christian organization?"

I uttered, "Yes, I figured that you weren't, but to answer your question, I would likely share Christ with them."

Soon after that response, they called an end to the meeting and asked me to step outside so they could deliberate. I stood in the hallway, and in my mind was saying to myself, "Shoot, that would have been such a good job for the summer."

Two minutes went by, and I was asked to come back in. They only asked me two more questions. The first being, "When can you start?" And the second, "Do you have any friends like yourself? We need one more." I found out that even though Hollygrove was officially secular, the three in charge were Christians and very much wanted Christ to be shared with the children. For some of them, Christ was their only hope.

I called Ralph describing the job and asked if he wanted to be considered. He said, "Absolutely!" They conducted an interview with him but were already convinced he would work out. And they were right; he did.

Some of the basic benefits of this job included not only a good salary, but also free room and board only blocks away from one of the most famous places in the world, Hollywood and Vine. Another benefit was that many Hollywood celebrities or businesses often came by to donate time, money, or supplies to the home. I can't tell you how many gallons of ice cream were stored in our freezer. Ralph and I were encouraged to eat as much of it as possible before it got too old. As you can imagine, we gained a few pounds, but we were young.

Celebrity groups like The Monkees donated clothes which, obviously, could not fit any of the children. So, Hollygrove gave me the pick of the litter before carting them off to Goodwill or the Salvation Army. PC had begun to loosen the dress code for guys, so during the next year, I ended up being one of the trendiest dressers on campus, wearing un-Nazarene-like bell bottoms and funky tops.

Occasionally on the weekends, Ralph and I would walk up to the center of Hollywood and just hang out on Sunset Strip or Hollywood and Vine. As we walked the streets, we would see new music groups starting up like the Doors at the Whisky a Go-Go, or Ike and Tina Turner. Even the Beatles played one evening at the Hollywood Bowl. What a summer!

Hollywood, with all of its pizzazz, looked very exciting and attractive on the outside but was full of a lot of disgusting and detestable things. There were drugs of all kinds, profuse drunkenness, and boundless sexual promiscuity. Prostitution and homosexuality were rampant.

One evening when Ralph and I went up to share the Four Spiritual Laws with people on Sunset Strip, we met with little success. As the evening wore down, we decided to get something to eat at a nearby café called the Silver Chalice. It was about eight in the evening. At first, I did not notice anything unusual about the café, but Ralph did. While we were eating, Ralph said, "Look around, Kent."

I did and saw that every single person in the café was male; there was not one female anywhere.

Ralph whispered, "This is a homosexual hangout we walked into." There were men at tables, men as waiters, and a whole counter filled with about 20 guys.

"Ralph, let's get out of here."

On the way out, while paying the bill, Ralph pinched me like a man would pinch a woman inappropriately. Immediately there was a whole host of men looking at me because of what Ralph did.

I exclaimed, "Why did you do that?"

Ralph laughed, "Just having fun, cutie!"

I countered, "You jerk!"

On a more positive and much more memorable note, we experienced some time with the Hollywood Chamber of Commerce when they came to Hollygrove one day to set up a trip for the kids to go to Disneyland. If that wasn't enough, they asked some of the runners-up in the Miss America Contest to help chaperone the kids on this trip. They needed at least two staff members from Hollygrove to go with them, so of course, Ralph and I were the first to raise our hands. Off we went to Disneyland with some Miss America contestants, and, oh yeah, the kids too. What a day we had! To top it off Miss Kentucky was assigned to me and a couple of kids. She was not only a *knock-out* but a very nice person, too, and a Christian as I remember.

Later in the summer, some of these gals came back and volunteered to take the kids to the beach, so once again Ralph and I stepped forward to drive the bus and go along. These beautiful girls in their bikinis were quite a sight to behold. I couldn't help but think at the time of the Scripture, *"If God is for you, who can be against you."* I probably misapplied this verse that day, but at least I quoted it. Doesn't that count a little? As we headed back home from Huntington Beach, Ralph turned to me and said, "Aren't we the luckiest guys on earth

More importantly, while at Hollygrove that summer, we really got to know Bob, Margaret, and Eleanor. Each of them was very mature in their faith and had a great deal of knowledge about how to apply God's grace. They willingly taught us all that we wanted to know about it, including a very important promise laid out in the Scriptures we never forgot. The promise is that God will never leave nor forsake us no matter what we do - good, bad, or in-between. That certainly helped when getting acquainted with Miss Kentucky during one of the best summers of my life.

Junior Year

"PUUSSSHH – When seventeen Pasadena College students left on a 23 day European Tour, they didn't realize the consequences of an economy tour. On the second morning they had to push the bus to start it as they left Belgium en route to the Rhine Valley in Germany. The eight nation tour offered six units credit in History, but none in Physical Fitness."

Chapter 19

Viktor Frankl

Due to the many absences from chapel by so many students such as myself, a new system of attendance was introduced my junior year. Instead of signup sheets or being checked from the back to see if you were where you were supposed to be, they came up with a system that was hard to breach. It worked well for quite a while, so I gave up and attended chapels my junior year. Besides, my attitude had changed a little toward chapel because of the faith experiences I had with Campus Crusade for Christ the year before. But even though I was growing in my faith and maturity, there was still a cavern of free-spiritedness in me that loved to stick it to Nazarene legalism when possible.

During the first few months of chapel, some of the speakers who were brought in were quite good but not all by any means. I think the school tried to improve chapels, but they still brought in a lot of guys that were boring, out of touch, or focused on guilt themes.

However, one chapel I will never forget, and that would not be forgotten by the whole school for quite a while, was a speaker from the Holocaust, Viktor Frankl. It was amazing that a small

What was I Thinking?

college like ours could line up someone like him. To this day, I am not sure how they did it. To prepare for this chapel, the school gave out some suggested reading material about Frankl. I guess I missed their memo because it would have altered my agenda that day.

Because of several poor chapel speakers in a row, I decided to enliven things a little. I had procured a few cherry bombs (loud firecrackers) but did not know how to set them off without being near the spot. Knowing my dilemma, one of my free-spirit friends suggested I attach a cigarette to the fuse and then light it. He said it would take about 15 minutes for the cigarette to burn down to the fuse. That sounded like a good plan, so I set about to make it happen, not knowing who the speaker would be at chapel. I probably thought at the time it would be just another dip-stick Nazarene preacher.

My seat in chapel was in the front row. In fact, some of those guilty of missing chapels on a regular basis were strategically assigned to the front row. Before chapel, I went back to the men's bathroom which was located at the back. I tied two cherry bombs together with two cigarettes. I put them under a metal trash can, so if anyone came in during the blast, they would not be hurt. I lit the cigarettes and proceeded to my seat. Somehow, a few in the front knew something was up. I guess they picked up on the familiar look on my face when something was about to happen.

Viktor Frankl started out well and was obviously an outstanding speaker with a lot of great stories and content. I was feeling rather guilty as he spoke because I knew what was about to happen unless somehow the fuse didn't work. I was hoping it didn't. As Frankl moved into an experience where the German's shot some of their victims, sure enough, the two cherry bombs went off like a cannon. Frankl immediately ducked underneath the podium. I had to fake like I was shocked. Two or three teachers in charge of the chapel rushed back to the bathroom to see who had done such a stupid stunt. There was no one to be found. The cherry bombs not only made a spectacular noise, but they also blew up all the evidence showing how they were set off.

When Frankl came up from behind the podium, he laughed, joked about it, and continued to share his story. He was great! Some thought I might have been responsible, but how could that be, when I was in the front row? I was never questioned about the incident. If I had been, I would have admitted my involvement. Even though I thought it was okay to do stuff like this in my cause against legalism, I knew it wasn't right to lie.

I wish I hadn't pulled this prank as Victor Frankl was worthy of greater respect then I gave him that day. Sorry, Viktor, shame on me!

Chapel bathroom where the cherry bombs went off!
(Picture taken in 2017)

Chapter 20

Victory at Sea

PC was short on dorm space, so they built a new one for all the guys who were upper classmen naming it Young Hall. It was finished just in time for my junior year. The old East Dorm where I began my first days at PC was torn down.

Wendell and I made plans over the summer to room with each other. I would have roomed with Ralph, but he wasn't sure he was coming back in the fall. He finally decided to do so, but it was at the last minute. It was too late to change my plans with Wendell, so Ralph ended up rooming with one of his old friends.

Wendell's dad, who was the pastor at LA First Nazarene, was all in favor of our rooming together for he had heard of all that went on during Easter week with Campus Crusade. His youth director, Sonny, shared the experience with him. Pastor Wellman also knew that Wendell had a tough beginning at PC and was hoping he'd room with someone who would be a good friend to him. Wendell did not always get along with the run-of-the-mill Nazarenes, so I fit in very well.

As time passed, Wendell and I did become the best of friends, proving that rooming together was a good thing. He was academically disciplined and gifted and talented in many ways, particularly in music and writing. This benefitted me greatly; I will expound upon that later. I helped him learn how to relax and not take things so seriously. In a way, Wendell's melancholic and sometimes dark view of life was met with my more phlegmatic and humorous approach. It was a good match, for we each strengthened the other.

At the time, Wendell did not have much of a grasp on God's grace and forgiveness, and his intelligence did not allow him to opt for legalism which he grew up around in the Nazarene church. Sad to say, a legalism that continued to be quite prevalent at PC.

Neither of us could stand this approach to Christianity. It was summarily nothing more than living life according to outward appearance and rules not found in the Scripture. Wendell's usual response to legalism was open and sarcastic criticism. Mine was to ignore or play jokes on those practicing it.

I not only played jokes on the Nazarene faithful who practiced this kind of Christianity, I sometimes did the same with those who bugged me. An example is a guy next door in our dorm. Even though these rooms were brand new, you could hear just about everything going on from one room to the next as the walls were thin and not well insulated. Next to our room was one of those Nazarene students who followed all of the rules but did not study a lick. In fact, he played his music and talked very loud into the night as the rest of us tried to study or sleep.

We tried to talk with him a few times about keeping it down but to no avail, so I decided to make a real impression on him. I borrowed a record album called *Victory at Sea*. The first part of the album starts with a battleship shooting off its big guns on deck as a part of the overture. If you turned up the volume, it could be quite startling but very inspiring. Boom, it would go! Then another boom. . . and another. . . and another. It was loud. I took this record and an old record player of mine and put it under this guy's bed on a day I actually saw him go to class (he rarely did). I ran an extension cord from under his bed to a wall in his room which led to a window. Then I ran the cord through the window into my room in a way so he wouldn't notice. It obviously worked because when Wendell and I got up early the next morning, we were able to plug the cord into one of our outlets with great effect. When the electricity hit the record player under the guy's bed, and the needle started doing its thing on the album, boom it went! Boom, boom, and boom, it repeated! It was much louder than I had anticipated. In fact, it woke up that whole side of the dorm.

Mr. Victory at Sea's room next door in Young Hall, minus a broken window!

The guy, from his roommate's testimony, went from a sound sleep to an immediate leap toward the window. He actually broke the window. Wendell and I made an impression on him, as well as the rest of the dorm, that morning. I then took my record player out, telling him more was ahead if he didn't hold it down. He checked out of school at the end of the week, and we never saw him again. We were all glad, including his roommate.

Not because of this incident alone, but rather, because of our on-going resistance against the school's legalism, some dorm supervisors put us and others of like-minds on an unannounced watch list. (At least, that is what I felt and thought at the time.) Their goal was to catch us doing something that could give the school administration reason to discipline, suspend, or even expel us.

This played out when those in charge of the front desk in the dorm took things into their own hands. I am not sure they were given permission to do what they did. In each room at the dorm, there was an intercom connected to the front desk. No one had cell phones back then, and there weren't phones in the rooms. If you received a call, it would go through the front desk first. Then, they would call you on the intercom to come down and take the call. Those at the front desk could flip on the intercom to your room without you knowing it and listen to what was being said. The only reason we found this out was because Ralph and his roommate Bernie happened to walk by the front desk one night and noticed what they were doing. Ralph and Bernie realized that if they were doing this to us, then they probably were doing it to others as well. As a result, a few of us met at the Grinder, a local café down the street, to talk about it. One of the guys said he could rig up a light on our intercoms that would indicate when they were listening. We had him do this immediately and as secretively as possible. When the light came on in our room, we had nothing to say but positive things about PC. When it was off, we talked freely. I guess we could have ended this right away by confronting these student leaders, but it was fun countering what they were doing.

Ralph and Bernie even went a step further. When the light came on in their room, they made up stories about some of the Nazarene faithful on campus. Consequently, rumors flowed rampantly around campus for a while because of the conversations that were being listened to. When the light went on in their room, they would pretend to be having a prayer meeting for some of the leaders on campus who were drinking, breaking school rules, or having sex.

These student leaders finally got caught and were "reprimanded" by being moved to other duties. After that, listening in on students stopped for good, when other higher-ups entered the picture and squashed it, realizing the school could get sued for such an invasion of privacy.

My friendship with Wendell continued to develop during my junior year. I had great appreciation for his mind and the way he went about doing his school work. In many ways, he forced me to be a much better student then what I had been. To do this, Wendell used his masterful art of sarcasm. If he wanted to make a point with me, he said it in a cynical way, meaning quite the opposite. For example, many times when I began to leave the room to play basketball after studying just a few minutes, he would say, "Well, Kent, working on those basketball skills? That will get you to the NBA." He didn't have to say much more. I would promptly drop my basketball, go back to my desk, and do the work I was supposed to get done.

In the last months before school ended, he also taught me how to think critically, write, and study for tests. I helped Wendell, too. Sometimes, he would get very dark and depressed, especially after others criticized him. I would not let him dwell in his darkness very long; I would counter with many positive things. In the end, he helped me with my life, and I helped him with his. It was a good friendship; one the Lord created for us both.

Wendell and I a year later

Chapter 21

Fall Crusade

Right after school began, Ralph and I considered the idea of getting a Campus Crusade ministry going at PC. This idea appealed to us because of the great experience we had with Crusade during Easter week of last year. However, Campus Crusade had never established a ministry on a Christian campus before as its focus had always been toward secular campuses.

In late September, we approached Crusade's leadership with an idea to have them train and support PC students to reach Pasadena City College students with the Gospel. Pasadena City College was a totally secular campus with lots of non-Christians. They agreed and got the ball rolling to make it happen.

Linus Morris, whom I met and worked with at Balboa week during the spring, ended up being the Crusade contact who would oversee this venture. Since he was fairly busy overseeing UCLA, he could only meet with Ralph and me periodically, to show us what to do and how to do it. And so we began.

At first, we started with a number of meetings to teach PC students who were interested how to share the Four Spiritual Laws and the Spirit-Filled Life. These two subjects had little booklets that went with them explaining how to come to Christ and how to begin living the Christian life. Having these booklets was very helpful, because if you *blew it* while presenting the message to other students, at least you could leave the booklets with them.

After Crusade saw our sincere interest to move forward, they took an additional step and sent one of their most popular speakers, Dick Day, to help carry out the first part of our training. When we heard he was coming, Ralph and I set up more meetings on campus and advertised them like crazy. The result was that many students showed up, thrilling and surprising me at the same time. I had thought PC was only filled with legalistic Christians who were not interested in sharing their faith with others. But I was wrong; on that evening at least 200 came.

Dick Day was phenomenal in all of his presentations, and when they concluded, we were able to get over 50 students to go to Pasadena City College to share the Gospel. I filmed what we did, and I shared later in other invitational meetings to get additional students involved. I felt if they saw what we were doing and how easy it was, they would jump on board. They didn't, but at least 50 of us did.

Over the next few months, we continued to share the Gospel. As we did, many students on our campus talked about it. Eventually, the buzz subsided, making what we were doing "old hat" or past news.

To my knowledge, there had never been anything done like this on any of the Nazarene campuses, and I am unaware of it taking place since. The typical Nazarene way of sharing the Gospel was to bring non-Christians to church and then depend upon the pastor to preach the salvation message. At the end, those interested in being saved were asked to come forward and pray at the altar. The problem with this was that non-Christians were rarely brought to church. When they did show up, they were uncomfortable about walking forward in front of others they did not know. Those that actually came forward were only Nazarenes feeling guilty about something, or to be saved once again. Sadder still is that only the preachers ended up being the ones to share the salvation message, the rest simply sat and watched.

The entire year on campus was amazing, sharing Christ with others and learning how to trust God through Crusade's Spirit-Filled Life booklet made life on campus good, even in the midst of an ever-present legalism. However, no matter what we did, many still did not believe that what we were doing was real. This was especially evident in the continued rejection of guys like Ralph whose lives had really changed. It was rumored that our transformations were only on the surface and used to camouflage our sins and true intentions.

Two such skeptics and doubters were Kathy and Karina. I had dated Kathy a couple of times, but there was no attraction between us, nor any real friendship. Ralph really liked Karina and wanted to date her badly. However, she did not dig Ralph because of his past reputation for wildness.

I came up with the idea of a beach trip to allow us the opportunity to counter their skepticism. We invited them to the beach to talk about some of our experiences with Crusade. Kathy didn't really want to go but said she would. She was only going to provide some support for Karina, who was curious and really did want to go to see what we had to say.

When we got to the beach, Karina and Kathy asked several questions about our experiences with Campus Crusade for Christ. They didn't believe the stories being circulated around school about what we were doing, especially those connected to Ralph. Only Karina's questions were sincere. Kathy's seemed to be more of "I could care less." She wasn't a legalistic Nazarene by any means; she was somewhere in the middle, not too hot or too cold.

What was I Thinking?

While sitting and talking at Will Roger's State Beach, all of us munched on some potato chips Ralph brought. Out of the corner of my eye, I noticed a guy reading a book about 20 yards away. As Ralph continued to explain and defend what he was doing, I got up and walked over to this guy. I did not do this to prove anything to the girls but just felt compelled to do so. Besides, I had already done this a few other times while working with Campus Crusade. I introduced myself to him, got to know him a little, and then finally asked, "Have you ever heard of the Four Spiritual Laws?"

During this time, Karina and Kathy were curious about what I was doing. They asked Ralph, "What is Kent up to?"

He responded, "Kent is probably doing what we have been talking about and accomplishing all year."

They replied, "What's that?"

"Let's wait and let him explain when he returns."

Meanwhile, I was going through the Four Spiritual Laws with this guy, and at the end, I asked him if there was any reason he would not want to accept Christ into his life? It was obvious the Spirit was moving; you could see it in his heart and on his face as we were talking. He immediately answered, "There is no reason not to." So we prayed, and he accepted Christ.

I got his name and number to do some follow-up. Linus, who I met through Campus Crusade and who had trained me, told me always to do this. It was just as important to follow up and disciple someone as it was to lead them to Christ. The young guy, who was a student at UCLA, had to hurry off, for a class starting in about an hour. Before he sped off, I took him over to meet Karina, Kathy, and Ralph. As he left, he said, "Thank you so much for what you shared with me."

When I sat down, Kathy asked, "What was that all about?"

"Kathy," I said, "that guy just accepted Christ."

Karina immediately jumped in and said, "You mean he just received Christ because of what you shared with him?"

"Yeah, that is exactly what happened."

"Really? Wow!"

Then I said, "This is what Ralph, a few others at school and I have learned this year. If you put your faith in God, take a chance, and present the Gospel to whoever comes your way then anything can happen, even belief in Christ."

As our time came to an end, Kathy was not convinced, but Karina was. Years later, well after our time at school had come and gone, I ran across Karina. She was making her life count by sharing Christ with others. As for Linus, who trained me so well, he was just at my house in Boise last week, some 50 years later following up on what I was doing.

Linus and his wife Sharon

Chapter 22

Sunset Boulevard

Ralph and I had some incredible experiences after Easter week of our sophomore year. Our Crusade ministry the next fall at school was also an overall success. Both of us, along with others, had really grown to trust God with just about everything during this time in our lives. Yet, we wanted to do more for we were so alive in our spirits. I think freedom from the guilt that legalism had put on us was the reason for our new energy. With the Campus Crusade people we met, there was no such guilt, only reassurance, compassion, and understanding, even when one blew it.

Because of this awakening, I began to look at God differently. Instead of viewing Him as tracking, catching, and condemning me for every sin I committed (or thought I committed), I now saw God as loving me no matter what. I also noticed as I trusted Him more, my struggle against legalism was supplanted for a while with a new courage to present the Gospel to non-Christians. I wanted to reach out to those completely devoid of God, specifically, those who roamed the streets of Hollywood during that 60s era.

Instead of going to church on Sunday mornings, which had mostly been a drag (LA First was an exception), Ralph and I went to Hollywood every Saturday night to share our faith with those who walked or hung out on Sunset Strip. The Strip was about a mile and a half long and was fairly wild. Hippies pretty much dominated the streets preaching peace, free love, and unreserved acceptance. The young people who lived all along the Strip opened their apartments to anyone and everyone. Girls "made love" with guys they just met because this was the "loving" thing to do.

This open culture actually worked to our advantage when sharing the Gospel as long as we focused on the theme of the love of Christ. This would get us an opening to share at least. Ralph and I usually arrived on the Strip at about 11:00 every Saturday night and came home around 5:00 Sunday morning. We were too tired to attend church

On our walks, we would go by places like the Whisky A Go-Go, a very popular hangout. One night when we were there, they introduced a guy named Jim Morrison and The Doors. Sound familiar? We did not do any drinking. We could have and not been caught, but we were reluctant because of the commitment we made to PC that year. When we ordered drinks, we only ordered ones that looked like alcoholic drinks. We would then strike up conversations about God's love and the love He demonstrated by sending His own Son to die for our sins. This message and its emphasis were usually well received.

Sometimes we got invited over to an apartment to talk further. A few of the invitations led to some of the girls offering to sleep with us, but we declined to their surprise. Each apartment had its own psychedelic look with the tie-dyed shirts, strobe lights, and kids sleeping everywhere. And even though we went to great lengths to present the Gospel, very few ever responded. Most were experimenting with a new drug called LSD, and one of its side effects was that you could not remember anything after taking it. We were offered some LSD on a few occasions, but said, "No way!" In fact, none of the drugs offered to us was ever tempting. Another drug came along that was deemed "safe" at the time, almost as safe as marijuana, and that was cocaine. What fools they were as cocaine ended up to be one of the most addictive and worst drugs ever.

The hippie, peace, and love movement did not last long-just a few years in the 60s. By the beginning of the 70s, it was buried and replaced by the Jesus Movement. This movement went on for a while longer and was full of ex-hippie types who had received Christ in the 60s.

During the time of my Sunset Strip ministry, I will never forget when several of my old Nazarene buddies came to me again and cautioned me to quit what I was doing. They said if I continued to hang out with such low-lives and sinners, then I would become just like them. Some of these guys were the ones who refused to join in with Crusade and take the Gospel to the students at Pasadena City College. I replied calmly, "Thank you, but for the moment, my church is out on Sunset Blvd. on Saturday nights." From that point on, there was a great distance between us. It was too bad because, at one time, I was very close to these guys. From then on, we only addressed each other in superficial ways at school until we all graduated.

Regrettably, some of these old friends had their own struggles with sin and only had a legalistic view of God when trying to cope. There were situations of sexual indiscretion and a couple of lost marriages. Ralph and I are still with the same girls we met and married over 45 years ago.

Chapter 23

Made Up Grades

Toward the end of the school year, my roommate, Wendell, helped me with a class we had together taught by Dr. Gray. Dr. Gray was the model Nazarene professor at the school. He was smart, well educated, a great father, and a dedicated member of the Nazarene church. He even went on church mission trips with young Nazarenes to reach out and minister to Native Americans still living on reservations. Yet, in all that was good about him, I felt he had an incredible weakness. He did not treat all students on campus in a like manner.

This played out in some of his classes where he seemingly gave greater preference and grade reward to those dedicated to the Nazarene church. This put me in a dilemma as I had gone to the Nazarene church for years, was a Christian, but I was openly and honestly not a Nazarene at heart. It appeared to me and quite a few others taking Dr. Gray's course that he was not fair in his grading. With few exceptions, the Nazarene faithful seemed to get better grades on his subjective tests frequently. Grades for research papers and subjective tests were also at his complete discretion.

After a few months of class, Dr. Gray started getting complaints from students about his grading. They declared he was not just, objective, or impartial. As the final exam approached, which would count for a huge part of your class grade, he announced that more objective questions would be added to the test to guarantee fairness. That seemed reasonable and was appreciated, especially among the non-Nazarenes who felt they were being shafted.

Everyone studied hard for this last exam; study groups were formed. To help me, Wendell, who had done quite well in the class so far, prepped me as he did himself. We were ready! The day came, and the exam was taken. Afterward, there was exhilaration as everyone felt they had aced the final, even the non-Nazarenes. Yet, it took an unusually long period of time to get the test results out and the final grades in for the class. The longer it took, the more nervous many became, especially the non-Nazarenes.

Then finally, well after the time the grades should have been posted, they came out. It was unbelievable. Those who thought they had aced the exam were disappointed and disgusted. How could this be? Many queried, "How can our grades on the final be exactly the same as the grades leading up to it?" Worse yet, the final grade for the course saw no improvement. It just did not make sense for a long while, until later it was reported that Dr. Gray had inadvertently misplaced the tests and could not find them anywhere. Rather than admitting this and re-administering the exam, he made up the grades according to what had been scored on previous tests and papers. It was also learned that he did not consult anyone before doing this. He just did it.

Needless to say, this did not inspire any of the non-Nazarenes in Dr. Gray's class to ever consider the Nazarene take on Christianity. What he did was not only unethical and wrong, it smacked of being discriminatory toward them. There was nothing that could be done about it, though, because he was too powerful and influential in the school. What was done stayed done!

The point of sharing this story is that none of us live the Christian life without making mistakes, errors in judgment, and even outright sinning. However, when we do blow it (as Dr. Gray did), all we need do is seek His forgiveness and apply the grace God has already given us.

You may be surprised to hear that I liked Dr. Gray, even though I was one of the victims of his grading. I liked him because when I went on some of those mission trips to the Indian reservations with him, I found Dr. Gray very kind, humble, and considerate. I only wished he could have been the same with our class. But all is forgiven. He is just as much under the grace of God as me.

Chapter 24

The Vietnam Draft

Sometime in late March, I got a draft notice to report for duty to the Armed Forces which would likely land me in Vietnam. However, the draft had a stipulation that if you had a certain grade point average (GPA), you could finish the school year. For me, everything depended upon my math class. If I had an "A" in this class, then I would have the overall GPA needed. To achieve an "A," I needed a favorable grade on a mid-semester test I had just taken. The only issue was that the grade I got gave me a 92.9% for the class; 93% was an "A." Right after getting my test back, I went to my professor and explained to him my situation. It wasn't unusual or inappropriate for a professor to round up a grade when it was this close. In fact, most would do this if it was 92.5 %. He would not budge or change anything. I couldn't believe it. When he told me his decision, it only made me more disgusted with the hardhearted legalism I often saw on campus with faculty like him. Therefore, my overall GPA ended up just barely short of the requirement. The Army didn't care; I was theirs as far as they were concerned.

Two Saturdays later, I reported for my physical with fear that I might eventually get shipped to Vietnam. As well, I stood to lose all of my credits for the semester. Yet, in the midst of this fear, I never lost my love for humor or my trust in God. I felt He would intervene somehow and get me through it all. My only regret, though, in what followed is that I was not the one who pulled off one of the funniest pranks ever.

When I arrived for my physical along with hundreds of other guys my age, we were asked to strip down to our shorts. The place we reported to was in downtown Los Angeles and looked like a typically gray, dark, and impersonal military building. At first, they took our temperatures, measured our heights, took our blood pressures, listened to our hearts, but then they asked us to drop our pants to check for hernias (and other things, too, I guess). It was all a little uncomfortable for most of us, but the Army didn't care. They finally asked us to give urine samples.

This is where things got funny because this whole experience was so sobering. While everyone was doing their urine samples, one of the guys in line was not paying attention to the instructions. So another guy near him told him he was supposed to go and take a dump (bowel movement), wrap it in some toilet paper, and then put it on the counter with the urine sample.  When he questioned doing this, he was told that some were asked to give urine samples and others dump samples; it was a random kind of thing. When he did it, we watched as the Army person receiving his sample said, "What's this?" Then, he opened it up. I can't repeat the expletive that came out of his mouth. This poor guy who gave the sample was duly chastised. Everyone in line busted up with laughter for a minute or two as it gave us all some relief from what we were experiencing.

After another couple of weeks, I received my classification letter from the draft; it read, "1A, available for military service."

However, only a few days later came an announcement that the GPA requirements were being done away with. Instead, if you had not missed a semester of college, you would be allowed to finish the school year. Fortunately, I had not missed a semester, so I was able to finish my junior year. As I reflect on this, I remember being thankful to the Lord for stepping in. I was not, however, thankful for my math professor who flunked his compassion exam.

The school year came to a close, and I somehow made it through the summer without hearing from the draft board. I finally heard from them in September just as my senior year began. The letter from them said that I was free to finish my senior year, but would have to report afterward. I was happy, to say the least, particularly to the Lord whom I felt stepped in and made this happen.

In June, after I graduated, I got a final draft letter telling me to report. In response, I wrote an appeal and basically said that God had told me that I was going to graduate school in Wyoming. I also told the draft board that I could have gotten a guaranteed deferment by going to seminary but just did not feel led to at this time. Did I really think they would consider this appeal? Probably not, but why not just tell the truth?

I heard nothing back from them throughout the summer. After checking in at graduate school, I got a note from the draft board saying that my appeal had been denied and that I should report for duty, but that I could appeal again if I chose. I did and said in my appeal, "Perhaps, you didn't understand that God had told me to go and finish graduate school." I didn't hear back from them again until after my first year of graduate school was completed

In the middle of the summer, while getting ready for my second year of graduate school, I received yet another notice saying that I had to report for duty and that my second appeal had been denied. At the end of this denial, they told me I still had the right to appeal their decision. I did, and for a third time, I explained to them God had told me to stay in graduate school. Amazingly, I did not hear from them again until that November. At this time, the draft put a lottery system into play where the lowest numbers would be the first drafted. I waited that fateful night of the drawing and got 227 as my number. This allowed me to finish my final year of graduate school because they only drafted 30 numbers a month. By the time I got home from school, they were up to 210 in the draft lottery, and I would have been in the next group to go. Before the next draw was made, the U.S. decided to pull out of Vietnam, and the draft was discontinued.

I guess they didn't understand that when God is in control, man isn't. For me, that meant that I was not going to Vietnam but graduate school, instead. For others who prayed and hoped with just as much fervor, it was His will they go and experience Vietnam. Neither path was greater or lesser than the other, just different for different reasons belonging to God.

Later on, I found out the reason for all the delays in responding to my appeals, delays that God knew and let happen. Evidently, there was corruption in my draft board forcing the federal government to step in and clean up the mess. Every time an appeal came in like mine, no matter what it said, it was put at the bottom of 2000 or so other appeals. It took at least five or six months to go through all of these appeals. God used this to keep me on track with what He wanted me to do. It did not include Vietnam.

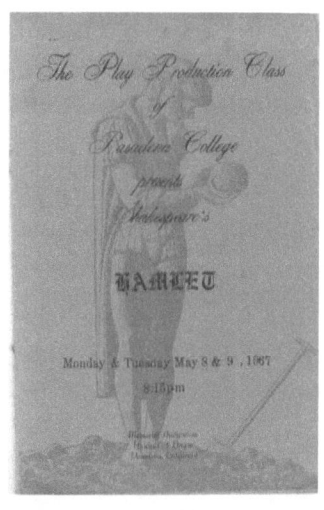

Chapter 25

Hamlet

One of the last classes I took in my junior year at PC was play production with Dr. Emmel. In my opinion, he was not only one of the best professors in the school but also one of the most mature and healthy Christians we had on campus. Granted, he was a Nazarene, but more than that, he totally understood God's grace and the appropriate role, rules and regulations should play in the Christian life. I took every class that he taught. He was a breath of fresh air. It was he who got me into graduate school.

The grade for this play production class was determined by how well you contributed toward producing a play. This involved possibly acting, creating and building sets, doing publicity, playing supportive roles in the production, or whatever was needed to make this play a success.

My roommate, Wendell, could not wait to sign up for the class. Many others wanted in the class as well, including free-spirit types and dedicated Nazarenes. Wendell hinted to me that Dr. Emmel really was intent on doing Shakespeare's *Hamlet*, but he wanted everyone in the class to have a say in the choosing of the play.

Wendell said, "Maybe, Kent, when the class gets together, and the subject comes up about which play to do, you could step forth and suggest *Hamlet*."

"No problem, Wendell. *Hamlet*, it is," I said.

The first day of class began with Dr. Emmel explaining all the good things we would learn as a class by doing a play together.

He said, "Not only will we be discovering different aspects of putting on a play, but we will be learning by doing, and that often is the best path to understanding. Therefore, we need to choose a play that is going to challenge us, stretch us, and be a production that the school will be proud of. Here are three possibilities: the first is *Our Town* by Thornton Wilder, the second is *Three Sisters* by Anton Chekhov, and the last is *Hamlet* by Shakespeare."

He explained the advantages and disadvantages of each play, but you could tell in his explanation that he was leaning toward *Hamlet*. He asked our opinion. A couple of students thought that *Our Town* would be good and another wanted *Three Sisters*. Dr. Emmel just listened.

I spoke up, "Seems to me that *Hamlet* has lots of parts and action, like sword fights, and I think *Hamlet* might draw a lot of guys and athletes into the audience."

Wendell spoke up with enthusiasm, "I agree!"

Anna and Stephanie said, "Yes, let's do *Hamlet*."

Dr. Emmel said, "*Hamlet* it is. There are swords, and there is a fight, but also, there are many other good things to learn by presenting this play. And it has a large cast."

On the way out of class, Wendell whispers to me, "You just got an "A" for the class no matter what part you get."

There were endless hours of rehearsals and meetings, but none of us griped about it. We really enjoyed not only working together but being with Dr. Emmel hour after hour.

The play was a total success, and one of the best plays PC had ever produced. Wendell and a few others did some great acting. He continued on with an acting and screenwriting career in Hollywood, which he is still doing today.

Regretfully, though, this play ended up to be Dr. Emmel's swan song to the school. He had just accepted a position at another university beginning that fall. We were sad when he told us at the end of the performance but glad for him at the same time.

Out of all of the classes at PC, this one, in my opinion, was the best portrait of what the school should have always been and looked like, including its leaders, professors, students, and other staff. The school leaders should have looked like Dr. Emmel, full of unconditional love and grace for every student no matter where they were with God or with life itself. Like the script which made *Hamlet* so popular, the doctrine of the school and church should also have been well-thought out, well-written, well-applied, and well-remembered. Students should have been more like what we experienced in that class with one another- pursuing the same goal, supportive of one another, and happy to be together.

Dr. Emmel and wife Naomi at my engagement party years later

Chapter 26

Karate and Final Exams

Finals week at the end of my junior year taught me how *not* to prepare for exams. I never again repeated this approach to studying. This includes my senior year and all of the graduate work I've done since. At the time, I knew in principle that these last exams were critical to my final grade in each class. That did not seem to faze me as I only began to prepare for finals the weekend before they were to be given.

I had another friend who also prepared at the last moment like me. His name was Lonnie, and he was from Montana. I met Lonnie about four months earlier in a rather unusual way. We should have never ended up being friends because of it, but we did. Surprisingly, Lonnie was a ministerial student. In most circles, ministerial students are nonviolent, but Lonnie wasn't. In fact, Lonnie was a bully. He often intimidated other students on campus and walked around with a very prideful swagger. He was rude to those he did not like or know. Sounds like a great minister, huh? As you might have guessed, I did not like him and kept my distance as much as possible.

One evening while I was standing in line at the school cafeteria, Lonnie burst in and promptly went to the head of the line.

He did not hesitate to push in front of me and even knocked me aside a little while doing so. In response, I took my right hand and cupped it as I had been taught in my karate class. I then hit him with my hand on the jugular vein in his neck. It was a lucky shot and did what it was intended to do, which is to paralyze an opponent's shoulders and arms temporarily. Immediately, Lonnie went limp and fell down to one knee. I followed up with a warning to never push me like that again. Embarrassingly, he limped out of the cafeteria, missing dinner altogether.

    I learned this karate move at Ed Parker's Karate School in Pasadena where both Ralph and I took classes. During our time there, Ed took a real liking to Ralph and me and sometimes put us in competition against other clubs. We were not black belts, by any means - not even close to it. Therefore, Ed usually refrained from putting us up against others that were above our level.

    I remember one time when he did, though. It was a competition we were to have with Chuck Norris' Karate Club. He is a famous actor in Hollywood you've probably seen on the screen as *Walker, Texas Ranger*. Chuck Norris brought some of his students to Ed's for a little competition one day. Guys from his club were paired with guys from ours. However, there was no one on Ralph's and my level with which to match up. Instead of just having us do nothing, Ed decided to see how Ralph and I would do against a couple of more advanced guys. After all, what could happen except a little embarrassment and some hurt? I can't remember how Ralph did, but I did not do so well at first with my opponent. He was landing blows right and left on me, and it got me a bit angry. Some people in life get scared when adverse things happen; others, like me, get angry. This has taken the Lord some years to root out of me. In my anger, I started to come back at this guy with the little skills I had. My aggressiveness caught him off guard, and he retreated. The contest was soon called to an end as it was getting testy. I remember that Chuck was not too happy with his guy, and Ed was expressionless, only giving me a wink of approval.

So, back to Lonnie, the strike on his neck was more effective because of the power I put into the blow than the technique. Nevertheless, it achieved its purpose.

From then on, Lonnie gave me a new degree of respect on campus and decided to make me a friend. He did not have many. In getting to know one another, he shared with me one of the main reasons he came to PC. It was because he was in trouble with the law at home.

I asked him, "What did you do, Lonnie?"

"Well, I was in a battle with a local rancher, and in revenge, I shot several of his livestock."

I was shocked. "You shot his livestock? Wow, now, that's heavy, Lonnie. I hope you asked for God's forgiveness."

I can't remember what he said.

What I do remember most about Lonnie, though, is the week we spent together studying for finals. We had the same classes, so studying together made sense. We decided to split up the work and share our notes with each other.

There were four days of exams and only two days leading up to those exams to get ready. I studied day and night for almost six days without sleeping, not even an hour. I was so behind in my preparation that sometimes I only had a day to get ready for one or two tests.

On the fourth night of this study marathon, without any sleep, I felt I couldn't make it any longer and shared this distress with Jed, another good friend of mine. Jed said he thought he had a solution. His mother had lost a lot of weight by taking certain prescribed diet pills. The only negative effect of these pills was that they kept her awake all day and night. She couldn't sleep a wink, so she stopped taking them. I asked Jed if he could get some of them for me. He said, "Sure, after all, they were prescribed and couldn't be that dangerous."

When I took the first pill, my eyes brightened, my energy jumped a level, and I was ready to go on with my studies. Every time I started to fade I took a pill, and boom, I was ready to go study some more.

I made it through finals and passed all of them, but on the sixth day, I crashed. And I mean crashed. I slept for 24 hours straight and then some. Lonnie did not do so well with his exams and ended up transferring to another school. I never saw him again. Years later it was rumored that he had to leave seminary because he got arrested for holding up a small convenience store. Evidently, his reason for robbing the store was to pay for his tuition. I could be wrong, but I don't think Lonnie was called to the ministry unless it was to a prison ministry.

One last note, I found out later that the pills I took were nothing more than a toned down version of Speed. It was later made illegal, even for diets. Thank God I did not take more of them than I did. He was protecting me even in this.

Chapter 27

Europe

After the school year ended, I had an opportunity to take six units of history in summer school by going on a European trip organized by PC. One of my favorite history professors was leading the tour. It seemed like a great opportunity to not only see Europe with some good friends but an easy six units to get out of the way in my history major. Jeff, one of my best friends, and Barbara were going on the trip. Barbara was the girl I dated for a short while in high school whose dad was high up in the Nazarene church and who I told at freshman registration that I thought she should have gone to UCLA and not PC.

There were 19 of us in all, and the trip only cost $800 for three weeks in Europe. My mother was pretty excited about me going to Europe, so she willingly flipped the bill for it. The trip, though, was almost canceled two weeks before we were to embark as evidently there had been some shady dealings with the company setting up the tour. At the last minute, it was reinstated (for us at least). There were many other groups set to go who lost most of their deposits in the process.

Friday night at 9:00 we flew out of LA International on American Airlines to New York and then to London. Our group was a mixture of both young and old, very Nazarene, middle-of-the-road Nazarene, and not Nazarene at all. Even so, we all got along pretty well as we traveled from one country to the next.

One of the challenges we faced each day was at mealtime. In every restaurant, whether for lunch or dinner, beer and wine went with the meal. Since we were from a Nazarene college, we asked them to remove the beer and wine and replace it with sparkling water or soda. They did so, with confused looks on their faces, and charged us accordingly.

The sites we visited during the day were remarkable. We learned a lot about the history of Europe by seeing them. But at the end of each day, all we wanted to do was kick-back and have some fun. Because we were Nazarenes, we were limited in what kind of fun we could have. We could not go have a beer at an outdoor café overlooking the Coliseum in Rome, for instance. We went to outdoor cafes anyway, drinking cokes and playing cards. Of course, we could not play games like poker or blackjack, as that was against the school rules. We played games like *Rook, War* or *Oh Hell* (with the same playing cards mind you) and with *Oh Hell*, we were encouraged to call it *Oh Heck* instead. After all, we were Nazarenes.

I'll never forget one of these evenings while in Rome when a bunch of guys gathered in my room and began wrestling. I guess we were not tired from the day but looking for something to do other than playing cards again. One of the guys on the trip, Gary, suggested we have a wrestling competition to break things up. Now, Gary had been in Circle "K" at school and definitely remembered the fun I made of him and other members. This made our relationship a little cool at first on the trip, but as we got to know each other, we became good friends, and all of that was forgotten.

As we began to set up the wrestling matches, Jeff and I were the first to go against each other. Jeff was tough to wrestle because he was so much bigger than me. After several minutes of going back and forth, a break in the action was called. Gary stepped in and coached how to get the advantage over Jeff. Who would know better than Gary, for he had been an all-state wrestler in high school. He told me to rush Jeff, get to his thighs, lift him up quickly, and throw him down. Seemed reasonable! When we resumed, I tried this, but while thrusting Jeff across the room and toward the window, both of us came close to falling out. That would not have been a good thing since my room was six stories up. Seeing this, Gary jumped into action and grabbed the two of us. Fortunately, he was fast enough and strong enough to pull us from harm's way. I don't think we would have fallen out, but it was close. Once again, God was looking out for me but this time through a new friend, one who had been in Circle "K" of all things. As the Scripture says in Psalm 139, "Each of us has just so many days here on earth, which was established before we were born." I am glad my last day wasn't that day. We took a permanent break from wrestling, not wanting to test the Lord's patience again. We went back to playing cards, turning to more competitive games like *Spoons*, *Old Maid*, and *Crazy Eights*.

While going from city to city on the bus, there was a lot of clowning and joking between us. We even gave pet names to one another. We called Bill *Gung-Ho*, for example, because no matter where we went, he was the first off the bus. We called Jeff *Gung-Heck* because he was the last out of the bus, wanting to take his time. There was a girl named Phyllis we gave the name *Radar Ears* because every time we began to lower our voices in the back of the bus to talk about something not so Nazarene, you could see her straining to hear what we said. This had a big impact on me after the trip was over.

On our last few excursions, I'll never forget my time with Barbara in Italy. I had not spent much time with her up until this point on the trip. We both decided to climb to the top of the Leaning

What was I Thinking?

Tower of Pisa, some eight stories high. When we got to the top, Barb startled me when she purposely swung out on one of the pillars, as if to throw herself off the tower. There were no guardrails, so she could have easily been killed. She then swung back and was safe again.

I shouted at her, "Barb, what you are doing? Are you crazy?"

She replied back "Kent, it just seemed like a good idea at the moment."

I then took her by the arm and escorted her down to the bottom floor.

Barb was a very different girl. She was sometimes quite normal, shy, and conservative and then sometimes wild, adventuresome, and a risk-taker. That was the exciting thing about her; you just never knew which person was going to show up. After we graduated from PC, I heard that they found a tumor close to her brain, which might have accounted for some of Barb's swings in behavior. They operated successfully.

On the last day of our trip we were in London and actually saw Queen Elizabeth. In the evening, we were all on our own for dinner. Barb, a few others, and I went to a Chinese restaurant. The first thing the waiter said when he served us was, "What would you like to drink?"

Without hesitation, Barb responded, "I'll have a Martini."

Another ordered a beer, and yet another ordered a mixed drink. I hesitated because I knew that if we were ever caught drinking, even on a trip like this, we would be disciplined or even dismissed from the school. While hesitating to make my decision,

Barb encouraged me to order a drink, so I did and totally enjoyed it and the rest of the evening. Most of us had just one drink, but Barb had a few more and got a little tipsy.

The next day we flew back to New York. It was right during the great airline strike of 1966. We were lucky only to be stuck at the airport for about 12 hours. While waiting to fly out, we actually ran across Bob Hope. Even he was stuck.

After our return home, all we had to do for the class was write a paper on a subject pertaining to Europe. Everyone got a good grade on what they wrote; our professor was very generous.

About two weeks after the trip, I got a call from Dr. White, the President of PC. As I arrived, I said hello to Barb, who was just leaving his office. I knew immediately that something was up. While I was a bit fearful, Dr. White was someone I knew very well, for he and my dad served as Nazarene pastors together when they were young. Dr. White was always intelligent, compassionate, and accommodating, and he even helped me get into PC just the day before registration began in my freshman year. He also knew a lot about my family and what happened to it. When I was very young, my mom divorced my dad, which was unheard of for the Nazarene faithful and especially for its pastors. I think he always felt bad for me because of this.

When I entered his office, he immediately wanted to know how things were going and how my experience at school had been. I related a little about my time at PC, focusing only on the positive. Then, perhaps without knowing it, Dr. White lowered his voice a bit and told me he had a concern to share. I could tell by his face that he was pained with what he was about to say.

He said, "Kent, in respect to your trip to Europe, some troubling concerns have arisen."

"What are they?"

"Well, it has been reported that there were a few of you on the trip who took a drink, and as you know, that is grounds for discipline or even dismissal from school."

Immediately, I thought that this might have come from *Radar Ears*, the girl who strained to listen to everything said in confidence by us. However, this was just a guess, and I never did find out who reported what we had done to Dr. White.

Dr. White continued, "As President of the school, I am obligated to follow up on every rumor that comes to my office, especially if it has to do with drinking. Therefore, I have talked with the students who were reported to have been drinking. And so far it is just a rumor. Now I need to ask you if you drank on the trip. By the way, Kent, before you respond, I want to say how much I appreciate what you've done on campus, especially in bringing in a new fervor for evangelism through Campus Crusade for Christ. You have done very well; your dad would be proud of you."

I then answered, "Well, Dr. White, I did take a drink, but just one at the end of the trip." He looked at me and was very quiet.

He responded, "I figured you would tell the truth, even if it meant your possible dismissal." He was quiet again, contemplative, thinking for a minute or two. He did not follow up with any more questions, not even as to who else might have been involved.

Then he said, "Kent, I am going to have to put you on academic probation. When others come and ask what was done in this situation, I will tell them I have put certain students on probation."

I asked him what academic probation meant.

He said, "You will only be able to take 12 units in the fall semester."

I said, "Thank you, you have been very gracious."

And he responded, "Thank you, Kent. I am glad you are a part of our school."

I saw Barb afterward and told her what happened. She did not say anything in return.

Sad to say, that later on after she graduated, her entire family was killed in an airplane accident in Oregon. Barb lost her parents, sister, brother-in-law, and grandparents. I wrote her after that, telling her of my great sorrow. As far as I know, she never married and lived alone the rest of her life. She died a couple of years ago.

When the fall semester began for me at PC my senior year, I signed up for 17 units. I guess Dr. White had forgotten to tell those in charge of my probation because I was allowed to take them all.

Once again, God's grace abounded.

Jeff (hat) and I in Rome

What was I Thinking?

Senior Year

Jennifer and I at the student union coffee shop

Chapter 28

The Twenty Dollar Bill

In my senior year, I did not want to go back and live at home. What senior wants to stay at home during this phase of his college experience? Yet, I did not want to stay on campus anymore. My roommate, Wendell, had graduated and was headed to UCLA. Ralph, who had joined me at Hollygrove the year before and had helped me with Campus Crusade, had left to go to Nampa Nazarene in Idaho. Therefore, I did not know where I was going to stay, and then Hollygrove called and wanted to know if I could work for them during the school year. They offered a job that would allow me to go to school for most of the day, work with their kids in the late afternoons and weekends, and live at Hollygrove.

On the weekends, I was designated as a "house father" to eight of the boys. During the week, they were taken care of in a cottage of their own by a "house mother." She was a much older woman. My duties on the weekends included making sure the boys got up, got dressed, cleaned their rooms, and made it to the cafeteria for each of their meals. The recreation leader on duty during the weekends took care of the rest.

When school began, I got up early every morning and drove the Pasadena Freeway from Hollywood to PC. Due to my new schedule, and because Ralph was gone, I dropped my responsibilities on campus with Campus Crusade for Christ. This was probably a huge mistake. What I helped start the year before was more important to continue than getting my room and board taken care of for the year and a little extra cash. I made this mistake because I did not consult with the Lord in this decision. To me, it was just logical to go back to Hollygrove to get my basic needs taken care of even if it meant dropping the Campus Crusade ministry.

The fall seemed to start off well, but that did not last long. Eventually, every day became a grind. The excitement and fulfillment of meeting with those who helped plan and carry out evangelistic activities in my junior year were past history now. Fortunately, what I had learned about God's grace and forgiveness helped me greatly as I sought to work my way back to the center of the Lord's will. The greatest lesson of all was that no matter what I did or whatever decisions I made, whether good or bad, in His will or not, God still loved me and would never reject or leave me. That was an incredible change in my thinking. Before, I believed if I sinned or did not do God's will then He would forsake me for a long time and even take away my salvation if what I did was bad enough.

Nonetheless, I was at Hollygrove at the beginning of my senior year rather than doing Crusade ministry on campus. And, yes, I did minister to the young boys under my care. I also continued to learn about God's grace from the three directors at this children's home who knew it so well. But I was neither happy nor content. I even continued to make poor decisions, which sometimes follow after a first bad decision.

One of those bad decisions was in the area of drinking. I decided since PC was so far away from Hollywood that I might experiment with having a drink every once and a while. It certainly hadn't affected me much in Las Vegas with my step-dad or in Europe. So, why not? Who was looking? This decision came after one of my basketball games.

During those months at Hollygrove, I played for a basketball team in a Tuesday night league. None of the guys I played with had any relationship with PC and barely knew it even existed. After each game, it was their tradition to go out and get a beer. They always asked me to go, but I didn't. Then, one night after a lot of prodding, I decided to go with them. It wasn't wrong for me to do this because drinking a beer was wrong it was wrong because I had made a commitment to PC not to do this, along with other things like going to shows, dancing, etc. I had one beer with the guys, which didn't affect me; I had a second. . . and then a few more. Pretty soon I was a little woozy. Fortunately, the guys I was with were savvier about drinking than I was and got me home safely.

I woke up in the morning at my mom's house in Pasadena. Thankfully, there was no school that day. I did not feel very good physically and, definitely, not spiritually. I knew that I had not lost my salvation and that God had not abandoned me, but I still struggled mightily.

The next time I went out with the guys after a game, I passed on having a beer. I pretty well determined that I was not going to do that again. My refusal, with which I believe God was happy, actually opened up a ministry for me that evening. There was an older man at the bar next to me who was about my stepfather's age. He'd obviously had a few too many drinks and slurred his words as he asked why I wasn't drinking. I don't remember all that I said at first, but I did refuse the beer he ordered for me. I talked with him for a while until he got a little more sober. During our conversation, I shared with him my experience with God. Kind of amazing! Here I was in a bar where I probably shouldn't have been, wasn't drinking, and sharing the Gospel with someone like this guy. Crazy! At least, for the first time in a few months, I felt God taking full control of my life again. When I got up to leave, this old and fatherly type of man pulled out a $20 bill and gave it to me.

What was I Thinking?

It wasn't just any $20 bill. It was a special one made in 1928 with the words "gold currency" on it and because of this, it was considerably more valuable than just a regular $20 bill.

I hesitated to take it and said, "Why do you want to give this to me?"

The man responded, "I was saving this to give to my son, but he died a few months ago."

I replied, "I am so sorry. That must have been tough."

After hearing that, I for sure refused to take the $20 and told him, "No, it's not right for me to take it."

He insisted and then said, "I own a little hamburger stand in Pasadena not far from your school, and anytime you want to come by, you can have a free lunch or dinner."

Soon after, I left with the guys but with the full intention of returning the man's $20. I sought him out the next day at his restaurant. Before I could say anything, he immediately fixed me a cheeseburger, some fries, and a malt. While he cooked, I told him I was returning his $20 bill, which I didn't think he remembered giving to me the night before.

"I do remember," he said, and then strongly stated once again, "I want you to have it." He would not back down.

Then, out of the blue, he asked, "Have you ever been to a horse race?"

I said, "No, never," even though I had grown up only a few blocks from the Santa Anita Race Track.

He said to come tomorrow, and he would close up early and take me to a horse race at Santa Anita.

"Okay, I'll be here," thinking this is something he and his son used to do.

I showed up the next day and off we went over to the horse races in his car. I guessed by conversations that he had been a horse trainer at some point. He knew everything about the horses, and I watched him make one bet after another, picking winners in almost every race.

Before the last race of the afternoon, he asked, "Do you want to take a chance and bet on this race?"

"Yeah, why not? I don't have too much money, but I can bet at least two bucks."

"That's all you need, and here is the horse to bet on."

When I looked at the program, I said, "This horse is a long shot. Are you sure?"

"Bet on him. I know who trained this horse, what this horse has done in the past, and the rest he's had between races. He's going to win."

I bet my two bucks, and he bet $25, which was a lot of money back then.

The starting bell rang, and they were off. As the horses rounded the final turn, his horse came from almost last place to win. He was $250 richer, and I got 25 bucks. What an afternoon!

I only saw this guy one more time after that. I tried to find him to share more of the Gospel, but his restaurant had closed. At least, I was able to share a little bit of the Gospel with him. A little is better than none, isn't it?

At this point, I knew that staying on at Hollygrove the rest of my senior year was not going to work. If I was going to completely get back on track spiritually, then I had to leave. I did so right after Christmas.

Before sharing how the rest of the school year went, there are two other stories about Hollygrove worth mentioning.

The first concerns a young girl who had lived at Hollygrove during her elementary school years. Ralph told me about her when we worked at Hollygrove the year before.

He asked me, "Do you know who Norma Jean Baker is?"

"No, I don't. Who is she?"

"Marilyn Monroe and she once lived here long before we showed up."

To reside at Hollygrove meant you had a very rough childhood, if not an impossible one. It was a difficult place for Norma Jean to come to because it meant she could not live at home. I don't know who the supervisors were when Norma Jean was there, but if she had come during the 60's rather than the 30's, she would have been under the care of Margaret, one of the most loving women I have ever met or worked for. To be around Margaret for any length of time was to experience God's love, for she was full of it. What a difference that might have made in Norma Jean's life, what a difference!

Not surprisingly, Margaret also showed me God's love by spending time teaching me about His grace. She died a few years ago, and I wish I could have been there to celebrate her life. I did write about her from afar, as many others did. I am sure God let her hear all of our comments.

The second incident I want to share happened at Christmas, right before I left Hollygrove. I had just spent time buying Christmas gifts for the boys in my cottage, the ones I took care of on the weekends. This was fulfilling to a degree, but I wished I had a girlfriend to do the same for at this time of year. I thought it would be great to bring a girlfriend to Hollygrove and sit in the lobby where a beautiful Christmas tree was. The lobby was in the main building where the administrative staff worked, meals were eaten, meetings conducted, and visitors welcomed. At night the lobby was completely empty except for the Christmas tree.

I wondered who I would invite to see this tree. I did not have a special girlfriend at the time. As I thought more about it, I did have a friend from high school named Shannon. Maybe I could invite her, but then remembered she had stronger feelings for me than I did for her. That scared me a little; but no matter, it was Christmas, and I decided to invite her anyway. The plan was to go out for dinner, give her a gift, and then go to Hollygrove to sit by the Christmas tree. And who knows, maybe I would give her a little mistletoe kiss or two in the process. As I was sitting with her on the couch that evening, with my arm around her, looking at the Christmas tree, she suddenly pulled out a Christmas gift for me in return. I opened it, and it was a beautiful picture of her. I told her it was a very nice gift and thanked her.

At that point, I realized she was definitely more serious about me than I thought. After contemplating this for a minute or two, instead of kissing her as I planned, I asked her if she had ever heard of the Four Spiritual Laws. This was the introduction I had often used in Crusade to open up a conversation about Christ.

Shannon answered back, "No, I never have. I never thought there were four spiritual laws."

I then shared them with her. As I came to the end, Shannon said, "Well, thank you. That is really something."

I asked if there was any reason she would not want to accept Christ as Lord.

Shannon responded immediately, "No, nothing at all; I would like to receive Him. What do I do?"

I told her and then prayed with her. While it was happening, I had to laugh at myself. Here was a girl I brought to make-out with in a Christmas setting but led her to Christ instead. What was I thinking?

After I got Shannon home, I felt the Lord was happy with me for leading her to Him, especially on His birthday. Several months later, Shannon met the guy she would fall in love with and eventually marry. He was a Christian, so it was a perfect match; a believer marrying a believer.

So, I ended my time at Hollygrove. What started out as a mistake ended up being a great course correction. I give total credit to God for this. No matter what I did or how long it took to get back on track, He never left my side, never gave up on me, and never stopped forgiving me. That's grace in a nutshell.

Chapter 29

Dating at School in the Raucous 60s

Some of my best relationships at PC were with the girls that became my friends. With only one or two exceptions, I never went out with any one girl for more than three times. This was probably because I was just not interested at this time in finding a life's mate. I also had a very high ideal of the kind of girl I wanted to marry.

The only relationship that threw me off a little was with Toni, a girl I dated during the summer after my freshman year. I only had three dates with her, but I thought I was in love. She was beautiful, a former homecoming queen, very smart, and, best of all, not a Nazarene. I met her at the Boys' Club where I was working. She came one day as a volunteer, and we hit it off immediately. Toni was a senior in high school, and I think was enthralled with the idea of going out with an older guy. I wasn't bad looking, a college guy, and articulate, all of which drew her interest. On the third date I kissed her, but when I called Toni again, she indicated she was interested in someone else. I later heard that she married him.

I languished over Toni for months, infatuated to the nth degree. It was not until I talked with some of my friends that I began to get over her. They explained how little I knew about her to be in love and how I should play the love game if someone else like her came along again. In essence, they said, "Play hard to get and never show your true feelings until you are assured of her feelings toward you." As good and logical as this input seemed at the time, I received even better advice later on from guys I worked with in Campus Crusade. They told me to treat all girls like sisters in the Lord, so they could say to their future mates that you helped prepare them for their marriage day. Eventually, one of those sisters would end up being just the right one for me. With these two pieces of advice, one from my friends and the other from Crusade, I began to date with a new perspective.

I can't remember dating anyone during my sophomore year after Toni, but I did build some good friendships with girls on campus. And that is what girls became to me, friends, not someone to get into a long-term relationship with. From time-to-time, I would veer off from this and make out with a girl or two but would always treat them honorably. By the way, making out in those days was limited to kissing and really nothing more.

One of the difficulties with dating while at PC was with the limits and rules put on students by the school. We couldn't go to movies, dance, play cards, show physical affection, and, definitely couldn't go to places where alcohol was even thought to be served. Rock concerts were out, club-like places were out, and most activities on Sunset Strip and Hollywood were out. So, what do you do? Well, you could go to dinner, to a school basketball game, to a choir performance on campus, to a youth gathering at church, or to the student lounge to eat popcorn and watch TV. None of these were very exciting and, in fact, got down-right boring after a while!

In response to this dilemma, a few of us tried to think of some things we could do on a date. Surprisingly, we came up with 25 possible activities. We also decided that if we did them together it would make our dates all that much more fun. Some of those activities included dinner and miniature golf, dinner and bowling, dinner and a roller coaster ride, dinner at the beach, and even a picnic dinner at the top of a kid's playground spaceship. These were fun at first, but even these activities got a little dull after a while. We then decided to have parties at one of the apartments where, yes, dancing was going on but not drinking. As these parties developed, the goal eventually evolved into who could bring the prettiest girl.

After one of these parties, Ralph and I got an idea. It was sparked by a relationship I had with Bruce, Jennifer, Donna, and Glenda, friends of mine on campus.

Before I explain the idea Ralph and I came up with, let me give you a little background on these four friends of mine. Bruce and Jennifer were dating one another, and Donna and Glenda were like me, not interested or attached to anyone at the time. The relationship with all four was good for me because they taught me a lot about how girls think and operate. For instance, it was Bruce and Jennifer who told me how most girls approach sex, which I was getting quite interested in at the time. I say "most girls," because PC girls were not like most girls. Bruce and Jennifer confirmed or corrected what I knew, and filled in the gaps on what I did not know. They, along with Donna and Glenda, also told me about the unique emotions girls had in comparison to guys and what they felt and went through during their monthly periods. Bruce and Jennifer eventually married, but sadly, divorced years later. I still keep in touch with Jennifer and did a well with Bruce until he died recently of as stroke.

I loved hanging out with these friends, especially the three girls. I would go over at least once a week to Jennifer, Donna, and Glenda's dorm and we'd go out and have coffee together.

What was I Thinking?

When I arrived, I would speak into the dorm intercom and say, "Is Glenda there . . . or Donna . . . or even Jennifer . . . or how about all three?"

They would answer back in a sarcastic and funny way, "What do you want to talk about now, McClain?"

Everyone on their wing of the dorm could hear this conversation. There was not an intercom to each room like the boy's dorm, only an intercom to a whole floor. After a number of meetings together, we began to add a little something to each intercom conversation. Since all could hear, why not spice it up a little?

Typically, my new approach started with, "Jennifer, or Donna, or Glenda, its Kent! Are any of you there?"

They would scream back, "Its Keeent!" and come running down to the lounge.

They came down as they were, in curlers, bathrobes, or whatever. The other girls on their floor began to wonder about all of this and even inquired about the relationship we had with one another. After all, who rushes down to see a boy without first preparing oneself? It got to be more hilarious after each time.

Then, one morning between classes at the student union, I asked, "What are the girls saying in your dorm?"

They just laughed and said, "These girls are incredibly intrigued as to who you are and are making up all kinds of stories." We all laughed.

Then in another conversation, Jennifer told me, "It's too bad so many of the girls on my floor never have any dates. No one ever shows any interest in them at all. If someone would date one of them just one time, then maybe others would too."

This is where my idea with Ralph picks up. I suggested to him that for our next party we bring a couple of girls from Jennifer's dorm, specifically two who had never had a date yet.

I told Ralph, "I am sure Jennifer would help us select these girls. She is the one who really hinted at the idea, whether she knew it or not."

Ralph looked at me, paused for a moment, and said, "That's cool. Let's do it."

Later that week, I let Jennifer, Donna, and Glenda know what we were doing and why. They agreed to set the whole thing up and would also serve as our intentional gossipers in the process.

Ralph and I followed through and went over to the dorm on a designated evening during the week. At Jennifer, Donna, and Glenda's suggestion, we called Maggie and Beth on the intercom. They answered, but both wondered what in the world we were doing calling them. Of course, Jennifer and the girls were in the background watching this all unfold, ready to pounce in and make it happen should it falter at any point.

I asked, "Maggie, what are you doing on Friday night?"

She answered, "Nothing really, just ironing my clothes. That's the night I usually do it." Then, she hesitantly questioned, "Why? What are you doing?"

"Well, Maggie, Ralph and I would like to take you and your roommate to a party on Friday night. Are you free?"

There was a bit of silence for a minute, some whispering, and a lot of shuffling around in the background. Finally, she said, "Sure, both Beth and I would love to go, but are you sure you have the right floor?"

"Yep, for sure. Ralph and I will pick the two of you up at 6:00 if that's okay?"

"Oh, yeah, that's fine. We'll be ready."

When we showed up at the party with these girls, most of the guys could not believe it as they were focused on bringing the prettiest girls possible. Maggie and Beth were not the prettiest but might have been on the inside. We introduced them to everyone and treated them as any girls we would take out.

Jennifer and Donna were waiting back at the dorm to see if we really pulled this thing off. We told them what we did. The incredible thing about all of this is that these two girls started getting more dates after that. Jennifer and Donna told us it was because of what we did.

Later, when we got together with the guys from the party, they just looked at Ralph and me and said almost in unison, "You guys are really a piece of work. What will you do next?" Amazingly, what started out as somewhat of a lark ended up to be a ministry to these two girls. I only wish we had done it even more, for the reason of truly being good brothers in the Lord to them.

The rest of my dating experiences during my years at PC were fun, too. As I entered my senior year, I began to think a little more seriously about who I took out. One girl I dated, for instance, was very beautiful but didn't go to PC. She attended LA First, where I attended. Along with her good looks, Judy was incredibly open and honest about her life. Some guys were reluctant to date her because the fingers on one of her hands were deformed since birth. That did not bother me, and it definitely didn't bother her. In fact, from the get-go, she would take her hand and put it in mine as we walked. We had a good time on our dates together. A couple of years later, she met a guy and fell in love. They eventually became engaged, but a week before their wedding, they took a trip in a small airplane. It crashed. Both were killed. It was such a tragedy. At the funeral, which should have been their wedding day, a ring ceremony was performed even though both were in heaven. None of us ever forgot her or that day.

Another girl I dated was Tina. She was also from my church. She was cute, a good Christian, and did not go to PC, either. When I took Tina out, she wore the fashion of the day, including miniskirts which were the rage of the 60s. I didn't complain, nor did many of the guys when I took her to PC events and basketball games. She had great legs. There was a song the Beach Boys came out with during that time called *I Wish They All Could Be California Girls*. Tina was definitely one of them!

As cute and Californish as Tina was, none matched another girl I dated who attended UCLA. I met Laura at a party one evening. She was blond, sleek, funny, and as beautiful as a girl could be. In fact, she had recently been chosen as Miss Teenage Dream Girl. In the early 60s, there were a few beauty contests to see who some of the prettiest teenage girls were in America. Laura won one of those contests and was a *knockout*, to say the least.

As I remember, we were talking at this party and hitting it off quite well when Laura asked me, "Have you ever sparked?"

I joked, "No, I must have missed that at PC. Maybe you could help educate me." Meanwhile, I was thinking, "This may be the best night of my life."

She giggled, "Ok, I have some evergreen mints in my purse, and we are going sparking."

Wondering what this meant and without thinking (or praying), I exclaimed, "I am all in!"

She then said, "Let's go find a closet!"

"Yeah, of course, let's go find a closet."

Needless to say, I was a little overcome, but excitedly so, for this girl was incredibly beautiful, and a dark closet was exactly where I wanted to be with her. We got in the closet, and she put an evergreen mint in my hand and one in her mouth. She bit down on the mint with her mouth open, and amazingly, a spark came

out. I did the same with mine. We tried it a few more times, and then she whispered, "Now our breath is nice, clean, and fresh, and we can kiss." And we did. We went on a few more dates, but we did not seem to be on the same spiritual wavelength. Too bad! Even beauty loses its attraction after a while if there is no connection to Christ.

As my senior year came to a close, I dated other girls from school and church and even one through the summer. But it wasn't until I got to the University of Wyoming for graduate school that I began to date girls for longer periods of time. As I look back at my dating experiences, I was definitely not drawn to anyone at PC. This is probably because most of the girls at my school did not have a good grasp of God's grace, nor were they very Californish in their looks and demeanor. With the girls I did date, I saw that it was much better to treat them as sisters in the Lord, rather than play the game of hard to get with them. As the guys from Crusade told me, one of those sisters will end up to be yours one day. And that is exactly what happened when I met and married Myrna some years later.

Chapter 30

The Grand Canyon

When Ralph came back from Nampa Nazarene College, one of the first things we did was visit some of the kids from Hollygrove. Of course, the directors at Hollygrove were thrilled we would come back for a visit. They could tell we had a lasting love for these children who were wards of the court. As we were leaving, they said we could come back anytime and take the kids on trips to just about anywhere. On top of that, they would pay for it.

So we did. We took Matt and Ryan, two eleven-year-old boys from cottage six, to the Grand Canyon. We drove in Ralph's car which did not have air conditioning. When we got to Needles, the temperature was 115 degrees. So, I said to Ralph, "How are we ever going to make it through this stretch of the road? We are all burning up."

We saw a gas station with a little market, and we stopped. We checked the radiator and made sure it was full of fresh water. Next, we went to the market and bought five ten-pound bags of crushed ice. We put one on the front dashboard, and each of us put one in our laps. Then we took off. We made it through with flying colors, eating our ice and putting it on our bodies. By the time we got out of the Mojave Desert, all the ice had melted and dried.

When we got to the Grand Canyon, we pitched our tents. We hiked a lot, ate dinners over the campfire, and talked with the boys about their relationship with God. It was a great time for us, especially the boys who never had dads in their lives to do this with. At the end of the trip, we asked them if they wanted to invite Christ into their lives. They did, and so we prayed with them.

When these boys were in high school, Bob, one of the directors at Hollygrove, called me and said that Matt was really struggling with issues in his life. Bob suggested I write him a letter of encouragement. I did but cannot tell you exactly what I wrote. Yet, I am confident it said something about trusting God. It must have because Bob wrote back and said that Matt had made a turn around a short time after receiving the letter.

While at a Hollygrove reunion many years later, I walked into the room where some of these grownup kids were. Now in their thirties with families of their own, there was Matt and his young family. This huge guy, all 6' 5" inches of him, grabbed me and lifted me off the ground with a big hug. When he set me down, Matt said, "Thanks, Mr. McClain, you saved my life with that letter." Needless to say, I was humbled. I only wish now as I look back at my college days at PC that more of my experiences could have been like this one. However, I now understand that grasping God's grace takes time and is filled with errors in judgment, misinterpretations, and wrong applications, as was the case during my journey at PC.

Chapter 31

Sharing the Gospel with even the French

In my final semester, I decided that I would attend chapel and not make any more crazy excuses. Evidently, God's grace was beginning to make changes in me, even with something I did not like or respect.

During this semester, Sonny, the youth director and founder of the Something Singers at LA First Nazarene, wanted to get together to discuss something with me. We sat down to talk after a game of tennis. He wanted to know why I hadn't been at church for several Sundays.

Before I could answer, he went on to say, "I know you've been busy going to school and working at Hollygrove, but I need you to do something for me."

"What is that, Sonny?"

"I need someone to be president of the college class at church. I also need you to be more consistent with the Something Singers."

I told him, "I can be more consistent now since I quit my job at Hollygrove."

"That's great and what about taking on the leadership of the college group?"

"Sure, I'd love to get more involved at church, but I would like to share the leadership with my old roommate, Wendell, and his brother, Wes."

"Good, I'll leave it to you to work things out with Wendell and Wes."

Together, Wendell, Wes, and I began to lead the class. Instead of calling ourselves the three presidents of the Alphadian college class, we referred to ourselves as The Triumvirate. This was a model of leadership the ancient Romans used when three men held the same title or position. When we get together even today, which is about every two or three years, we still call ourselves by this name just for fun. We got along then and still do.

One of our first moves was to recruit more college-age students and young professionals, including friends from PC, who had about a 25-mile drive to our church. At the same time, I began to work more closely with Sonny as he gave me more and more responsibilities.

Part of these responsibilities was to help with the Something Singers tours. One of the most memorable tours for the groups was to Yosemite and San Francisco. In addition to the performances we looked forward to, we were excited and curious about the Haight Ashbury district we were to visit in San Francisco. At the time, this district was considered to be the center of the whole hippie movement.

On our way to San Francisco, we first made a stopover in Yosemite. As was typical of Sonny and the way he did ministry, we sometimes picked up young hitchhikers on our trips. As we helped them get to where they were headed, we also invited some to join us on our trip.

My extra role on this trip was that of the bus driver. I was able to do this because I had gotten my license to drive a bus for Hollygrove.

While on the way up to Yosemite on Highway 99, Sonny suddenly yelled out to me, "Let's pick up that guy and two gals ahead."

"Okay, Sonny, just try and let me know a little more in advance," as I hit the brakes.

"Gotcha, Mr. Bus Driver."

The three people we picked up were college-age French students touring the USA for the summer, doing it as economically as possible. They could speak English but with a definite accent. None of us knew French at all. They gladly got on our bus; we looked like a pretty safe ride. When we got to Yosemite with these three young people in tow, we did not hesitate to sing some of our tour songs by the campfire at night. Sonny also thought it would be good to share some of our testimonies since we had an audience. I helped with this as Sonny had hoped I would. There were no conversions that night, nor would there be for the remainder of the trip, but at least we tried.

Even though these three were young like us, they were different in a lot of ways. For instance, I remember during one of our hikes with them, the two girls decided to change their clothes in the middle of our trek down from Glacier Point. They were hot, sweaty, and tired like the rest of us, but without warning, they surprised us by changing right in front of us, taking off their shirts and bras. Then they put on something a little lighter to finish the hike. I was taken back at first but definitely not griping by any means.

Later, one of the others on the hike later said to me, "Wow, McClain, did you see that? What did you think?"

"I think maybe God is calling me to be a missionary to France; that's what I think." We both laughed!

Soon after, we left Yosemite and headed toward San Francisco. While driving down the mountains from Yosemite, I

What was I Thinking?

noticed the brakes on the bus were not working very well. In fact, the brakes didn't work at all on the last hill. Fortunately, this hill had no curves and was straight all the way to the bottom where the road was flat. I told no one of the problem but quietly, and hopefully without alarm, pumped the brakes to get life back in them.

When we got to the bottom, Sonny came over and questioned, "Weren't you going a little too fast coming down off those hills?"

"Yeah," I said in my typical nonchalant manner, "the brakes seemed to have burned out on us."

Sonny looked at me in wonderment and said, "Really!"

I replied, "No matter, Sonny, by the grace of God, we made it just fine." He said nothing but immediately had the brakes checked at the gas station up ahead. They were fixed, and we were on our way.

After we arrived in San Francisco, our group set things up and got ready to perform at a pavilion sponsored by a few churches. Our performance was very much like what we had done during Balboa week for Campus Crusade for Christ two years earlier. After the performance, the three young French people planned to leave us and head off to yet another destination in California. Before they left and said their final thanks and goodbyes, one of the girls wanted to talk with me a little, so I walked to the beach with her. I thought it might be about something we had said or sang in regards to God. As we got down to the sand, she began to take off her clothes, until I stopped her.

She said in her broken English, "Don't zee wants to haves sex withz me."

"No," sputtered out of my mouth, "this is not the right thing to do."

"So yous a good boy, huh?"

"Yeah, I guess, kind of, sort of." Then she put back on what she had taken off, and we walked back to the group. We never saw or heard from these three from France again. We tried to write them later on but met with no response. Nevertheless, God's presence and grace in my life were growing, enough to make a good decision when it mattered most.

Our mission for this trip continued on. We shared Christ with the hippies and druggies we ran across in San Francisco, particularly those in the Haight Ashbury district where most of them hung out. In our group was an African American girl who was a good friend of mine. Together, we thought we might draw some attention and more opportunities to talk with the hippies by walking arm in arm down the street. Unlike most in my generation at the time, hippies were very open to racially mixed relationships and marriages. Our walk together worked to some extent but not as much as we had anticipated.

At that time in San Francisco, Eldridge Cleaver was head of the Black Panthers and was causing a lot of havoc in the area for whites. Therefore, we had to be very careful and watchful for most of us were white. Fortunately, we never did run across Eldridge Cleaver and the Black Panthers; thank heavens! However, I did meet with him several years later after he became a Christian. In a very unusual and unplanned set of circumstances, we ended up having dinner together one evening when Eldridge was speaking at Peninsula Bible Church in Palo Alto, California, where I was the high school pastor. During that dinner conversation, we shared our common faith in Christ.

Isn't it amazing and typical of God to take someone we genuinely feared at one point and make them a brother in Christ down the road?

What was I Thinking?

Beautiful Yosemite Valley

Chapter 32

June 6th, 1968

During the last few months of school, I roomed with my good friend, Ben. We were getting along pretty well in our apartment until one night when I almost burned the place down. One Friday evening, Ben and I invited two friends over for dinner, and I was the designated cook. Bruce and Jennifer, who had given me great advice about girls, were our guests. While fixing dinner, I learned the hard way that it is a good thing to clean your oven from time to time. Since moving in with Ben, I had never cleaned the oven, not even once. So quite naturally, grease dripped down, collected, and spread itself out. When I put the hamburgers into the oven, there was so much grease inside that when I opened it to see how they were cooking, the whole oven lit up and caught on fire.

During this time, Ben, Bruce, and Jennifer were in the living room watching the California primary election returns. They were all for Eugene McCarthy or Robert Kennedy to be the democratic nominee. The kitchen was situated in such a way that you could see what was going on from the living room. When I opened the oven door in a somewhat darkened kitchen, the flames rushed out and reflected on my face. Bruce saw this first and immediately yelled out, "Are you ok in there?"

I uttered back, "I think dinner is going to be a bit delayed."

Jennifer then asked, "Is there anything I can do to help?"

I didn't answer her, but asked Ben instead, "Do you know where a fire extinguisher is? I think I may need it."

All three immediately jumped up and ran toward the kitchen. I started to fill a pan of water to throw on the fire when Ben yelled, "Don't do that! It will only make it worse!"

With the flames gaining momentum, I took the dry potato flakes I was going to have with our meal and threw them onto the growing blaze. Praise God, the potato flakes worked and smothered the fire. However, now the mashed potatoes were all over the oven and were not edible. It was going to be quite a cleanup, so Ben and I decided to put off the task until the next day. Isn't that what college guys do?

Instead of burgers and instant potatoes for dinner, Ben took over and fixed a couple of sandwiches for us; we were too poor to go out for dinner. As we ate and talked, we began to laugh about the whole incident. Jennifer said, "And, Kent, when the fire was burning, which we could see reflected on your face, all you could say was that dinner was going to be a bit delayed?" We laughed more and ended up having a great evening anyway.

As Bruce and Jennifer got up to leave, I blurted out a prediction about the primary election. I said that Robert Kennedy would be assassinated before night's end. I don't know why I made such a prediction. I guess just seeing him on TV and remembering how his brother Jack Kennedy was killed caused me to say what I did. When Ben and I woke up the next morning that is exactly what had happened. Robert Kennedy had been shot at the Ambassador Hotel in downtown LA. We were shocked and greatly saddened, for we really liked him.

I drove that morning to LA First where Sonny had provided a small office for me. He wanted to prepare me to take over his job for the coming summer while he was going to be a camp director at Forest Home. The church was in favor of him doing this as long as he had a good replacement. They were happy Sonny picked me and agreed. Nevertheless, as I sat in my office getting ready to prepare a Bible lesson for the high school group on Sunday morning, I heard sirens going back and forth all day. The church sat between the Ambassador Hotel where Kennedy was shot and the hospital where he was taken.

While I sat in my office, I surmised by all of the commotion going on outside that Kennedy had probably died. He did die that day, June 6th, 1968, a terrible day. Soon after his death, I got a call from Jeff, one of my schoolmates. He exclaimed rather excitedly, "Kent, do you know who that guy was who shot Kennedy?"

"Yes, Sirhan something."

Jeff immediately answered back, "Sirhan Sirhan is his name, and he only lived a couple of blocks from my house."

"Wow, that's amazing, Jeff."

Jeff went on, "He also attended the Nazarene church we went to when we were young. Can you believe that?"

"No, I can't."

Jeff continued, "He was probably in one of our Sunday school classes."

"Wait a minute, Jeff. I do remember a guy with a name like that; he was kind of a weird dude as I remember."

"Isn't that amazing, Kent, that we might have known the guy who killed Robert Kennedy? I've got to go now; there is an FBI agent at my door. For some reason, they are all over my neighborhood collecting information about this jerk."

"Let me know what they say. It is too bad, though, the church couldn't have had more of an influence on Sirhan."

Chapter 33

Over and Done

After I graduated from PC, Sonny left for Forest Home, a very popular and renowned Christian camp in Southern California. I spent the summer as a substitute youth director. Amazingly, the Nazarene District Superintendent offered me a ministry license because of my new position. I say "amazingly" because during my four years at PC, I had hardly been a proponent of the Nazarene approach to the Christian faith. Nevertheless I took it. I don't know if having the license helped me much in carrying out my summer ministry, but it was the first of several such credentials that would follow in the years to come.

While at LA First that summer, I had the opportunity to teach other young people about God's grace, which I had discovered during my years at PC. I taught the high school department every week and continued to work with college students at church. The Something Singers were put on hold until Sonny returned; yet, some of the church socials, gatherings, and trips in which they participated continued. I lived in Sonny's house while he was gone. It was convenient and economical for me and also helpful to him. I took care of his yard, collected his mail, watered his wife's flowers, and watched over the place. His wife Linda actually wrote to me on

Facebook the other day and asked me how I got raspberry stains all over her nice towels back then.

I said, "Linda, are you joking? That was over 50 years ago!"

She quipped, "I was just kidding; we loved having you stay and take care of our place the way you did."

"Good, I will pass that testimonial on to my wife, who does not always think that I am the neatest person."

At the end of the summer, right before Sonny was to return, I organized and put together a very special trip to Yosemite. It was the spiritual highlight of my whole summer. There were between 20 to 30 of us who went, and during our time at this fantastic national park, we hiked, cooked meals together, had morning devotions, and openly shared our lives with one another. In the evenings at the campfire, I taught parts of the book of Romans, one of the great passages of Scripture that highlights the grace of God. Even Sonny's brother, Ron, helped with this teaching. In preparation, Ron and I met together each day to discuss Romans. We were always on the same wavelength which made the teaching that much better. Ron later became the pastor of one of the largest Nazarene churches in California, and through the years, we'd still get together from time to time to talk about the old days at LA First. Sad to say, at least for those left behind, Ron recently went to be with the Lord. He died of cancer.

As the trip wound down, a girl Ralph had been dating wanted to join us the last couple of days of the trip. I was okay with this, so Ralph arranged for her to drive his car up to our campsite. However, two days before the trip ended, a Park Ranger put a note on my windshield to call Memorial Hospital in Bakersfield. There were no cell phones in those days, so I had to find a landline in the park to find out what this was all about. When I called, I found out that Ralph's girlfriend had rolled his VW bug several times on Hwy 99 outside of Bakersfield. She was hurt and unconscious. I immediately told Ralph and let him take my car to Bakersfield as soon as he could get packed. For whatever reason, the girl's mother and sister could not be contacted, and the father had been out of the picture for years. Ralph took off, and we all prayed for her and Ralph.

Meanwhile, everyone started packing to go home. On the last day before we left, I let everyone do what they wanted or hike wherever they wanted. The younger ones, especially the girls, had to have an older partner or two with them before leaving camp. When everyone was set, I took off on my own hike to Hidden Falls, a place I had been before on other trips. I knew this part of my life was coming to an end. My time at PC was over and done, as was my time in California. After the trip, I would head off to the University of Wyoming to attend graduate school.

As I reached the bottom of Hidden Falls, I lay down on some soft ground with my eyes directed toward the sky. I began to say to the Lord, "Thank you for all that You have taught me over the last four years. Thank you for teaching me about Your grace. Thank you for getting me through PC, and thank you for paving the path to a place like Wyoming."

I felt the Lord say back, "My pleasure, Kent, my pleasure, and always remember I will never abandon or forsake you, no matter what." And He never has, not even once!

I walked back to camp and finished the last night with everyone singing and sharing. The next morning we took off on the bus, but as we passed Bakersfield, I decided to join Ralph. There were plenty of adults on the bus to take over in my absence, and everyone agreed it was the right thing to do. After a couple of days in Bakersfield, Ralph's girlfriend regained consciousness and started to recover. It turned out okay. Praise God, it all turned out okay.

It turned out okay for me, too. PC is where I learned of God's loving, forgiving, healing, and ceaseless ocean of grace in a pond of legalism.

Hidden Falls

Final Thoughts

The antagonist in the PC story was not so much the Nazarene students, administrators, professors, or pastors that I encountered or knew, for many of them were very kind and good people. The antagonist was the legalism that seemed to flow from many of their hearts and minds and dominated the philosophy and theology of the school and church.

In an attempt to live out the righteousness that was supposed to come from Christ, in my opinion, they turned to a form of legalism to perfect their righteousness. Such legalism says, "I will prove to God that I can live out this righteousness and demonstrate to others that I am being successful doing it." This approach always fails because it is a righteousness built on the individual and not God. He will have nothing to do with any righteousness that does not come directly and entirely from Him because our righteousness falls too far short of God's perfect righteousness.

For those steeped in legalism, as many were at PC, the more rules they could create, live by, and carry out in front of others, the better they felt about themselves as Christians. This is probably why a bulk of Nazarene students couldn't share Christ with others outside of their own faith because they couldn't relate to those, not like themselves. It is too bad because the Christian life was never meant to be a system of rules to follow but a life filled with His love and grace.

After I graduated from PC, a few of the free-spirits I felt comfortable around did come to know Christ. Not through me but through others God sent their way. Unfortunately, I've also heard through the years that many, who just went along with the legalism on campus, without ever questioning it, did not fare so well. Some grew cold in their faith and ended up doing very little for the kingdom, never leading anyone to Christ. Some became totally secular and numb toward God and the church. Others became problems in their churches, causing a lot of havoc and division. And, sad to say, others completely rejected God and became agnostics or atheists.

On a good note, there were those, too, at my school who were able to jettison the legalism by which they were influenced. To do so, many had to join independent churches or churches from other denominations where legalism was not prevalent. Several also stayed on with the Nazarene denomination to try and make changes from within. I know a few Nazarene pastors, professors, and friends who did just that and should be applauded for hanging in there.

I posted the question at the beginning of my PC story, *"What was I thinking?"* But really the question should have been, *"What was God thinking?"* when He put me at a Nazarene college? I had a choice to go to Pasadena City College where I was already registered. At the city college, I would have likely played basketball, done my regular humanity studies (less Bible courses), transferred to a state college, and followed a typical career. I probably would have gone to church, a different one, and even been serious about my relationship with God. But had I gone that way, I might never have grasped God's grace as I did by going to PC. God knew the best path for me, and it was PC. Since then, I have grown in His grace and taught others to do the same in many of my ministries. I feel fortunate to have served as a pastor, youth and children's minister, teacher, and Christian school superintendent over the years.

Do I still sin? Do I still disappoint God? Do I still make fun of Nazarene legalists from time to time? You bet. But I am getting better because God is the One at work within me. I will never be completely without sin all at once, which I jokingly referred to as being "simonized" (chapter 12), but He is making me a little less sinful every day. That is what sanctification is all about.

Before I end, here is how I define God's grace in my life: His complete forgiveness for all of my sins, those in the past, present, and future. I received His grace when I put my faith in Him and asked for forgiveness. At that moment, God's grace kicked into my life and became an ocean of forgiveness and mercy. Because of the vastness and depth of God's grace, I could throw everything into this ocean, even the worst that I did. Each time, I watched it disappear and sink forever.

In my mind's eye, the Lord would come and say, "Good job, nice casting of that junk you were holding on to. You're forgiven, always will be, so let's move on. We've got quite a journey ahead of us."

By the way, I did better on future term papers, although *The Lives of the Brown Bear and Polar Bear* was my favorite. A few degrees later I perhaps showed at least some improvement. Don't you think?

The following are some Scriptures that got me through PC. Many were gathered from those I met at Campus Crusade for Christ during those college years. These verses kept me steady back then. I pray they will do the same for you today.

"For by grace you have been saved through faith; and that not of yourselves, it is the gift of God; not as a result of works, so that no one may boast." Ephesians 2:8-9

"My sheep hear My voice, and I know them, and they follow Me; and I give eternal life to them, and they will never perish; and no one will snatch them out of My hand." John 10:27-28

"Not that I have already obtained it or have already become perfect, but I press on so that I may lay hold of that for which also I was laid hold of by Christ Jesus. Brethren, I do not regard myself as having laid hold of it yet; but one thing I do: forgetting what lies behind and reaching forward to what lies ahead." Philippians 3:12-13

"If we are faithless, He remains faithful, for He cannot deny Himself." II Timothy 2:13

"Therefore there is now no condemnation for those who are Christ Jesus." Romans 8:1

"For I am convinced that neither death, nor life, nor angels, nor principalities, nor things present, nor things to come, nor powers, nor height, nor depth, nor any other created thing, will be able to separate us from the love of God, which is in Christ Jesus our Lord." Romans 8:38-39

"Be strong and courageous, do not be afraid or tremble at them, for the Lord your God is the one who goes with you. He will not fail you or forsake you." Deuteronomy 31:6

... lo, I am with you always, even to the end of the age. Matthew 28:20

How precious also are Your thoughts to me, O God! How vast is the sum of them! If I should count them, they would outnumber the sand. Psalm 139:17-18

... "My grace is sufficient for you, for My power is perfected in your weakness" Therefore I am well content with my own weaknesses, insults, distresses, persecutions, and difficulties, for Christ's sake; when I am weak, then I am strong. II Corinthians 12:9-10

Other books by Kent McClain
    Teachable Moments available on Amazon
    Sowing Teachable Moments Year One available on Amazon

Articles and devotions by Kent at www.tmoments.com

www.ingramcontent.com/pod-product-compliance
Lightning Source LLC
Chambersburg PA
CBHW021441080526
44588CB00009B/627